Peter Stone, the only writer to win a Tony, an Oscar, and an Emmy, won his most recent Tony Award for Best Musical for *Titanic*. His musicals *1776* and *The Will Rogers Follies* won both the Tony and the New York Drama Critics Circle awards. He also won a Tony for his musical *Woman of the Year*. Additional Broadway credits include the musicals *My One and Only*, *Sugar*, *Two by Two*, and his collaboration with Erich Maria Remarque on the play *Full Circle*. The author of more than two dozen feature films, he won an Academy Award for his screenplay for *Father Goose*, an Edgar (Mystery Writers of America Award) for his film *Charade*, and a Christopher Award for the screen adaptation of *1776*. Among his other films are *The Taking of Pelham 1-2-3*, *Mirage*, *Arabesque*, *Sweet Charity*, *Skin Game*, *Who's Killing the Great Chefs of Europe?*, and *Just Cause*. Writing for television, he won an Emmy Award for an episode of the acclaimed series *The Defenders*. He has been president of the Dramatists Guild, the national society of playwrights, composers, and lyricists, since 1981.

Sherman Edwards was an ex-history teacher and successful songwriter who wrote dozens of top-ten songs, including "Wonderful, Wonderful," "See You in September," "Johnny Get Angry," and "Broken-Hearted Melody." His original conception of *1776* was derived from his love for both the men and the period in which they lived. The result was a combination of his avid interest in history (having majored in it at New York and Cornell universities) and his talents as a composer-lyricist. He was rewarded in 1969 with both a New York Drama Critics Award and a Tony Award for Best Musical for *1776*, as well as the Tony Award for Best Music and Lyrics. As a pianist, he was associated with Benny Goodman, Tommy Dorsey, and Louis Armstrong and appeared in concert with many of the jazz greats. Mr. Edwards died in 1981.

1776

A MUSICAL PLAY

(*Based on a conception of* SHERMAN EDWARDS)

Book by PETER STONE

Music and Lyrics by SHERMAN EDWARDS

Samer Zoukari
Gr.5
Ms.Thompson

PENGUIN BOOKS

PENGUIN BOOKS
Published by the Penguin Group
Penguin Group (USA) Inc., 375 Hudson Street, New York, New York 10014, U.S.A.
Penguin Group (Canada), 90 Eglinton Avenue East, Suite 700, Toronto, Ontario,
Canada M4P 2Y3 (a division of Pearson Penguin Canada Inc.)
Penguin Books Ltd, 80 Strand, London WC2R 0RL, England
Penguin Ireland, 25 St Stephen's Green, Dublin 2, Ireland (a division of Penguin Books Ltd)
Penguin Group (Australia), 250 Camberwell Road, Camberwell, Victoria 3124,
Australia (a division of Pearson Australia Group Pty Ltd)
Penguin Books India Pvt Ltd, 11 Community Centre, Panchsheel Park,
New Delhi – 110 017, India
Penguin Group (NZ), 67 Apollo Drive, Rosedale, North Shore 0745,
Auckland, New Zealand (a division of Pearson New Zealand Ltd)
Penguin Books (South Africa) (Pty) Ltd, 24 Sturdee Avenue, Rosebank,
Johannesburg 2196, South Africa

Penguin Books Ltd, Registered Offices: 80 Strand, London WC2R 0RL, England

First published in the United States of America by The Viking Press 1970
Published simultaneously in a Viking Compass Edition
Published in Penguin Books 1976

20 19 18

1776 text copyright © Sherman Edwards, 1964
1776 text copyright © Peter Stone, 1969
Lyrics copyright © Sherman Edwards, 1964, 1968, 1969
Historical Notes copyright © Sherman Edwards and Peter Stone, 1970
All rights reserved

LIBRARY OF CONGRESS CATALOGING IN PUBLICATION DATA:
Edwards, Sherman.
1776: a musical play.
Reprint of the ed. published by The Viking Press, New York.
Bibliography: p. 174.
1. Musical revues, comedies, etc.—Librettos.
I. Stone, Peter, 1930–
1776.   II. Title.
[ML50.E268s52   1976]
782.8'1'2   76-40099
ISBN 978-0-14-048139-6

Printed in the United States of America
Set in Linotype Times Roman

CONTENTS

STUART OSTROW *Presents*

1776

Music and Lyrics by SHERMAN EDWARDS
Book by PETER STONE
Based on a conception of Sherman Edwards

Scenery and lighting by Jo Mielziner
Costumes by Patricia Zipprodt
Musical direction and dance arrangements
   by Peter Howard
Orchestrations by Eddie Sauter
Vocal arrangements by Elise Bretton
Musical numbers staged by ONNA WHITE
Directed by PETER HUNT

1776 was first presented at the Forty-Sixth Street
Theatre on March 16, 1969.

ORIGINAL CAST

JOHN HANCOCK	David Ford
JOSIAH BARTLETT	Paul-David Richards
JOHN ADAMS	William Daniels
STEPHEN HOPKINS	Roy Poole
ROGER SHERMAN	David Vosburgh
LEWIS MORRIS	Ronald Kross
ROBERT LIVINGSTON	Henry Le Clair
JOHN WITHERSPOON	Edmund Lyndeck
BENJAMIN FRANKLIN	Howard Da Silva
JOHN DICKINSON	Paul Hecht
JAMES WILSON	Emory Bass
CAESAR RODNEY	Robert Gaus
THOMAS MCKEAN	Bruce MacKay
GEORGE READ	Duane Bodin
SAMUEL CHASE	Philip Polito
RICHARD HENRY LEE	Ronald Holgate
THOMAS JEFFERSON	Ken Howard
JOSEPH HEWES	Charles Rule
EDWARD RUTLEDGE	Clifford David
LYMAN HALL	Jonathan Moore
CHARLES THOMSON	Ralston Hill
ANDREW MCNAIR	William Duell
ABIGAIL ADAMS	Virginia Vestoff
MARTHA JEFFERSON	Betty Buckley
A LEATHER APRON	B. J. Slater
A PAINTER	William Duell
A COURIER	Scott Jarvis

CAST OF CHARACTERS

Members of the Continental Congress

President
JOHN HANCOCK

New Hampshire
DR. JOSIAH BARTLETT

Massachusetts
JOHN ADAMS

Rhode Island
STEPHEN HOPKINS

Connecticut
ROGER SHERMAN

New York
LEWIS MORRIS
ROBERT LIVINGSTON

New Jersey
REVEREND JOHN WITHERSPOON

Pennsylvania
BENJAMIN FRANKLIN
JOHN DICKINSON
JAMES WILSON

Delaware
CAESAR RODNEY
COLONEL THOMAS McKEAN
GEORGE READ

Maryland

SAMUEL CHASE

Virginia

RICHARD HENRY LEE

THOMAS JEFFERSON

North Carolina

JOSEPH HEWES

South Carolina

EDWARD RUTLEDGE

Georgia

DR. LYMAN HALL

Secretary

CHARLES THOMSON

Custodian and bell-ringer

ANDREW MCNAIR

ABIGAIL ADAMS

MARTHA JEFFERSON

A LEATHER APRON

A PAINTER

A COURIER

THE PLACE

A single setting representing the Chamber and an Anteroom of the Continental Congress; a Mall, High Street, and Thomas Jefferson's room, in Philadelphia; and certain reaches of John Adams' mind.

THE TIME

May, June, and July, 1776.

THE SCENES

1. The Chamber of the Continental Congress
2. The Mall
3. The Chamber
4. Thomas Jefferson's room and High Street
5. The Chamber
6. A Congressional Anteroom
7. The Chamber

The action is continuous, without intermission.

M USICAL NUMBERS

S C E N E 1

"Sit Down, John": John Adams and the Congress

"Piddle, Twiddle, and Resolve": Adams

"Till Then": John and Abigail Adams

S C E N E 2

"The Lees of Old Virginia": Lee, Franklin, and Adams

S C E N E 3

"But, Mr. Adams—": Adams, Franklin, Jefferson, Sherman, and Livingston

S C E N E 4

"Yours, Yours, Yours": John and Abigail Adams

"He Plays the Violin": Martha Jefferson, Franklin, and Adams

S C E N E 5

"Cool, Cool Considerate Men": Dickinson and the Conservatives

"Momma, Look Sharp": Courier, McNair, and Leather Apron

S C E N E 6

"The Egg": Franklin, Adams, and Jefferson

S C E N E 7

"Molasses to Rum": Rutledge

"Yours, Yours, Yours" (Reprise): Abigail Adams

"Is Anybody There?": Adams

SCENE 1

In front of the curtain.

JOHN ADAMS:

I have come to the conclusion that one useless man is called a disgrace, that two are called a law firm, and that three or more become a congress. And by God, I have had *this* Congress! For ten years King George and his Parliament have gulled, cullied, and diddled these Colonies with their illegal taxes— Stamp Acts, Townshend Acts, Sugar Acts, *Tea* Acts—and when we *dared* stand up like men they stopped our trade, seized our ships, blockaded our ports, burned our towns, *and* spilled our blood— and still this Congress won't grant any of my proposals on Independence even so much as the courtesy of open debate! Good God, what in hell are they waiting for?

The curtain flies up to reveal the Chamber of the Second Continental Congress in Philadelphia. At rise, Congress is in session, sweltering in the heat of a premature summer's evening. A large day-by-day wall calendar reads: "MAY 8."

CONGRESS:
singing:

Sit down, John!
Sit down, John!
For God's sake, John
Sit down!

Sit down, John!
Sit down, John!
For God's sake, John.
Sit down!

VOICE:

    Someone ought to open up a window!

CONGRESS:

    It's ninety degrees!
    Have mercy, John, please!
    It's hot as Hell in
    Philadel-phia!

TWO VOICES:

    Someone ought to open up a window!

JOHN:

    I say "Vote Yes!
        Vote Yes!"
      Vote for independency!

CONGRESS A:

    Someone ought to open up a window!

JOHN:

    I say "Vote Yes!"

CONGRESS:

    Sit down, John!

JOHN:

    Vote for independency!

VOICE FROM CONGRESS B:

    Someone ought to open up a window!

CONGRESS B:

    No! No! No!
    Too many flies!
    Too many flies!

CONGRESS A:

    But it's hot as Hell in
    Philadel-phia!

VOICES FROM CONGRESS A:
  Are you going to open up a window?

CONGRESS A:
  Can't we
  Compromise here?

JOHN:
  Vote Yes!

CONGRESS B:
  No, too many
  Flies here!

JOHN:
  Vote Yes!

CONGRESS, *full:*
  Oh, for God's sake, John,
  Sit down!

  They freeze.

JOHN, *speaks, roaring:*
  Good God!! Consider yourselves fortunate that you
  have John Adams to abuse, for no sane man would
  tolerate it!

CONGRESS, *resuming action, singing:*
  John, you're a bore!
  We've heard this before!
  Now, for God's sake, John,
  Sit down!

JOHN:
  I say, "Vote Yes!"

SOME VOICES:
  No!!

JOHN:
  Vote Yes!

CONGRESS, *full:*
>   *No!!*

JOHN:
>   Vote for
>   Independency!

CONGRESS A:
>   Someone ought to open up a window!

JOHN:
>   I say "Vote Yes!"

CONGRESS, *full:*
>   Sit down, John!

JOHN:
>   Vote for independency!!!

VOICE:
>   Will someone shut that man up!!

JOHN, *speaking:*
>   Never! Never! [*He storms from the Chamber, coming downstage, and looks to Heaven for guidance.*] Dear God! For one solid year they have been sitting there—for *one year! Doing nothing!*

Singing:

>   I do believe you've laid a curse on
>   North America!
>   A curse that we here now rehearse in
>   Philadelphia!
>   A second Flood, a simple famine,
>   Plagues of locusts everywhere,
>   Or a cataclysmic earthquake,
>   I'd accept with some despair.
>   But, no, you've sent us Congress—
>   Good God, Sir, was that fair?

I say this with humility in
Philadelphia!
We're your responsibility in
Philadelphia!
If you don't want to see us hanging
On some far-off British hill,
If you don't want the voice of independency
Forever still,
Then, God, Sir, get Thee to it,
For Congress never will!

You see we
    Piddle, twiddle, and resolve.
    Not one damned thing do we solve.
    Piddle, twiddle, and resolve.
    Nothing's ever solved in
    Foul, fetid, fuming, foggy, filthy
Philadelphia!

From the Chamber, rear, a Congressional voice can be heard.

VOICE:
Someone ought to open up a window!

JOHN, *speaking:*
Oh, shut up!

JOHN HANCOCK:
I now call the Congress' attention to the petition of Mr. Melchior Meng, who claims twenty dollars' compensation for his dead mule. It seems the animal was employed transporting luggage in the service of the Congress.

JAMES WILSON:
The question, then, would appear to be one of occasion, for if the mule expired not while carrying, but after being unloaded, then surely the beast dropped dead on its own time!

JOHN:

Good God!!

Singing:

They may sit here for years and years in
Philadelphia!
These indecisive grenadiers of
Philadelphia!
They can't agree on what is right or wrong
Or what is good or bad.
I'm convinced the only purpose
This Congress ever had
Was to gather here, specifically,
To drive John Adams mad!

You see we
    Piddle, twiddle, and resolve.
    Not one damned thing do we solve.
    Piddle, twiddle, and resolve
    Nothing's ever solved in
    Foul, fetid, fuming, foggy, filthy
Philadelphia—

*Abigail Adams, John's wife, a handsome woman
of thirty-two, now appears in John's imagination
and interrupts.*

ABIGAIL:

John, John!
Is that you carrying on, John?

JOHN, *speaking:*

Oh, Abigail! Abigail—I have such a desire to
knock heads together!

ABIGAIL:

I know, my dearest. I know. But that's because you
make everything so complicated. It's all quite
simple, really:

Singing:

Tell the Congress to declare
Independency!
Then sign your name, get out of there,
and hurry home to me!
Our children all have dysentery,
Little Tom keeps turning blue.
Little Abby has the measles
And I'm coming down with flu.
They say we may get smallpox—

JOHN, *speaking:*
Madame, what else is new?

Music under.
Abigail, in my last letter I told you that the King
has collected twelve thousand German mercenaries
to send against us. I asked you to organize the
ladies and make saltpetre for gunpowder. Have
you done as I asked?

ABIGAIL:
No, John, I have not.

JOHN:
Why have you not?

ABIGAIL:
Because you neglected to tell us how saltpetre is
made.

JOHN, *impatient:*
By treating sodium nitrate with potassium chloride,
of course!

ABIGAIL—*a woman:*
Oh, yes—of course.

JOHN:
Will it be done, then?

ABIGAIL:

I'm afraid we have a more urgent problem, John.

JOHN:

More urgent, Madame?

ABIGAIL, *singing:*

There's one thing every woman's missed in
Massachusetts Bay—
Don't smirk at me, you egotist, pay
Heed to what I say!
We've gone from Framingham to Boston
And cannot find a pin.
"Don't you know there is a war on?"
Says each tradesman with a grin.
Well!
We will not make saltpetre
Until you send us pins!

JOHN:

Pins, Madame? Saltpetre?

ABIGAIL:

Pins!

JOHN AND ABIGAIL, *alternating:*

Saltpetre!
           Pins!
Saltpetre!
           Pins!
Saltpetre!
           Pins!
'Petre!
           Pins!
'Petre!
           Pins!
'Petre!
           Pins!
'Petre!
           Pins!

JOHN, *speaking, beaten:*
    Done, Madame. Done.

ABIGAIL:
    Done, John. [*Smiling:*] *Hurry home, John.*

JOHN:
    As soon as I'm able.

ABIGAIL:
    Don't stop writing—it's all I have.

JOHN:
    Every day, my dearest friend.

ABIGAIL, *singing:*
    Till then . . .

ABIGAIL AND JOHN:
    Till then,
    I am, as I ever was, and ever shall be—
    Yours . . .
    Yours . . .
    Yours . . .
    Yours . . .
    Yours . . .

JOHN:
    Saltpetre. [*He throws a kiss.*] John.

ABIGAIL:
    Pins. [*She throws a kiss.*] Abigail.
    She goes.

CONGRESS, *singing:*
    For God's sake, John,
    Sit down!

    John turns, waves them off in disgust, then crosses.

JOHN, *calling:*
    Franklin!

SCENE 2

The Mall. Sunlight. Benjamin Franklin sits on a bench, having his portrait painted.

John discovers him.

JOHN:

Franklin! Where in God's name were you when I needed you?

FRANKLIN:

Right here, John, being preserved for posterity. Do y'like it?

JOHN, *after examining the painting carefully:*
It stinks.

The painter goes.

FRANKLIN:

As ever, the soul of tact.

JOHN:

The man's no Botticelli.

FRANKLIN:

And the subject's no Venus.

JOHN:

Franklin! You heard what I suffered in there?

FRANKLIN:

Heard? Of course I heard—along with the rest of Philadelphia. Lord, your voice is piercing, John!

JOHN:

I wish to heaven my arguments were. By God, Franklin, when will they make up their minds? With one hand they can raise an army, dispatch one of their own to lead it, and cheer the news from Bunker's Hill—while with the other they wave the olive branch, begging the King for a happy and permanent reconciliation. Why damn it, Fat George has declared us in rebellion—why in bloody hell can't *they?*

FRANKLIN:

John, really! You talk as if independence were the rule! *It's never been done before!* No colony has ever broken from the parent stem in the history of the world!

JOHN:

Dammit, Franklin, you make us sound treasonous!

FRANKLIN:

Do I? [*Thinking:*] Treason—"Treason is a charge invented by winners as an excuse for hanging the losers."

JOHN:

I have more to do than stand here listening to you quote yourself.

FRANKLIN:

No, that was a new one!

JOHN:

Dammit, Franklin, we're at war!

FRANKLIN:

To defend ourselves, nothing more. *We* expressed our displeasure, the English moved against us, and *we,* in turn, have resisted. Now our fellow Congressmen want to effect a reconciliation *before* it becomes a war.

JOHN:

Reconcilation my ass! The *people* want independence!

FRANKLIN:

The people have read Mr. Paine's *Common Sense*.
I doubt the Congress has. [*He studies him.*] John,
why don't you give it up? Nobody listens to you—
you're obnoxious and disliked.

JOHN:

I'm not promoting John Adams, I'm promoting independence.

FRANKLIN:

Evidently they cannot help connecting the two.

JOHN, *suspicious:*

What are you suggesting?

FRANKLIN:

Let someone else in Congress propose.

JOHN:

Never!

Franklin shrugs.

Who did you have in mind?

FRANKLIN:

I don't know. I really haven't given it much
thought.

*Richard Henry Lee, a tall, loose-jointed Virginian
aristocrat of forty-five, enters.*

LEE:

You sent for me, Benjamin?

JOHN, *looking at Lee, then at Franklin:*
Never!!

LEE:

Halloo, Johnny.

JOHN, *nodding:*
    Richard.

FRANKLIN:
    Richard, John and I need some advice.

LEE:
    If it's mine t'give, it's yours, y'know that.

FRANKLIN:
    Thank you, Richard. As you know, the cause that
    we support has come to a complete standstill.
    Now, why do you suppose that is?

LEE:
    Simple! Johnny, here, is obnoxious and disliked.

FRANKLIN:
    Yes, that's true. What's the solution, I wonder?

LEE—*it's obvious:*
    Get someone else in Congress to propose—

FRANKLIN:
    Richard, that's brilliant! Wasn't that brilliant, John?

JOHN, *dully:*
    Brilliant.

FRANKLIN:
    Yes. Now the question remains—who can it be?
    The man we need must belong to a delegation pub-
    licly committed to support independence, and at
    the present time only Massachusetts, New Hamp-
    shire, and Delaware have declared our way.

LEE:
    And Virginia, Benjy—don't forget Virginia.

FRANKLIN:
    Oh, I haven't, Richard—how could I? But strictly
    speaking, while Virginia's views on independence

arc well known, your legislature in Williamsburg
has never formally authorized its delegation here in
Congress to support the cause. Of course, if we
could think of a Virginian with enough influence
to go down there and persuade the House of Burgesses—

LEE:
Damn me if *I* haven't thought of someone!

FRANKLIN AND ADAMS, *together:*
Who?

LEE:
Me!

FRANKLIN:
Why didn't I think of that!

LEE:
I'll leave tonight—why, hell, right now, if y'like!
I'll stop off at Stratford just long enough to refresh
the missus, and then straight to the matter. Virginia, the land that gave us our glorious Commander-in-Chief—[*a short drum roll*]—George
Washington, will now give the continent its proposal on independence! And when Virginia proposes, the South is bound to follow, and where the
South goes the Middle Colonies go! Gentlemen, a
salute! To Virginia, the Mother of American Independence!

JOHN:
Incredible! We're free, and he hasn't even left yet!
[*To Lee:*] What makes you so sure you can do it?

Music begins.

LEE:
Hah!!

Singing:

My name is Richard Henry Lee!
Virginia is my home.
My name is Richard Henry Lee!
Virginia is my home,
And may my horses turn to glue
If I can't deliver up to you
A resolution—on independency!
For I am F.F.V.
The First Family
In the Sovereign Colony of Virginia.
The F.F.V.
The Oldest Family
In the oldest colony in America!

And may the British burn my land
If I can't deliver to your hand
A resolution—on independency!

Y'see it's—
Here a Lee
      There a Lee
      Everywhere a Lee, a Lee!

FRANKLIN AND LEE, *alternating:*
Social—
        LEE!
Political—
        LEE!
Financial—
        LEE!
Natural—
        LEE!
Internal—
        LEE!
External—
        LEE!

Fraternal—
>LEE!

E-ternal—
>LEE!

Together:

The F.F.V.
The First Family
In the Sovereign Colony of Virginia!

LEE:
>And may my wife refuse my bed
>If I can't deliver (as I said)
>A resolution—on independency!

JOHN, *speaking:*
>Spoken modest-*Lee*. God help us!

FRANKLIN:
>He will, John! He will!

LEE, *singing:*
>They say that God in Heaven
>Is everybody's God.

FRANKLIN:
>Amen!

LEE:
>I'll admit that God in Heaven
>Is everybody's God.
>But I tell y', John, with pride,
>God leans a little on the side
>Of the Lees! The Lees of old Virginia!
>Y'see it's
>Here a Lee, there a Lee
>Everywhere a Lee—a Lee!

FRANKLIN AND LEE:
>Here a Lee, there a Lee
>Everywhere a Lee—

LEE:

> Look out! There's
>> Arthur Lee!
>> "Bobby" Lee! . . . an'
>> General "Lighthorse" Harry Lee!
>> Jesse Lee!
>> Willie Lee!

FRANKLIN:

> And Richard H.—

LEE:

> *That's me!!*
> And may my blood stop running blue
> If I can't deliver up to you
> A resolution—on independency!
>
> *He begins strutting, a military cakewalk.*
>
> Yes sir, by God, it's
> Here a Lee!
> There a Lee!
> Come on, boys, join in with me!
>
> *They do, John reluctantly.*
>
> Here a Lee! There a Lee!

FRANKLIN, *speaking:*

> When do y'leave?

LEE, *singing:*

> Immediate-*Lee!*
> Here a Lee! There a Lee!

FRANKLIN, *speaking:*

> When will you return?

LEE, *singing:*

> Short-*Lee!*
> Here a Lee! There a Lee!

And I'll come back
Triumphant-*Lee!*

FRANKLIN AND JOHN:
Here a Lee! There a Lee!
Ev'rywhere a Lee! A Lee!

LEE:
Forrr-warr . . .
Ho-ooo!

*Lee struts off. Franklin and John follow him almost
as far as the wings, then drop out and return,
breathless but relieved.*

JOHN, *speaking:*
That was the most revolting display I ever witnessed.

FRANKLIN:
They're a warm-blooded people, Virginians!

JOHN:
Not him, Franklin—*you!* You and your infernal
obsession for deviousness! If you'd come right out
and asked him straight, he'd've been gone a half
hour ago!

FRANKLIN:
Cheer up, John. At this very moment our cause is
again riding high—sitting straight in the saddle
and in full gallop for Virginia!

Lee suddenly reappears.

LEE, *singing:*
—And our women are . . . serene . . .

JOHN, *speaking:*
Oh, good God!

LEE:
Full-bosomed . . .

FRANKLIN, *perking up:*
> Full-bosomed?

LEE:
> Full-bosomed, Benjy,
> Every one a queen! Why, they are . . .

> *Music in, at tempo.*

> —Lees! Dammit!
> The Lees of old Virginia! Yes, sir! By God!

Waving his riding crop, he parades around, followed by Franklin and John.

ALL:
> It's here a Lee!
> There a Lee!

LEE:
> Come on, John,
> Step live-a-*Lee!*

ALL:
> Here a Lee!
> There a Lee!
> Everywhere a Lee—a Lee!

Again Lee starts off, strutting between, but ahead of, John and Franklin, who are halfheartedly marching after him. Suddenly Lee has still another afterthought and turns back to express it—but John and Franklin are ready for him this time, hooking his arms as he passes between them, and dragging the surprised and frustrated Virginian off backwards.

SCENE 3

The Chamber.

Featured prominently, rear, is a tally board. Under three main headings (YEA, NAY, and ABSTAIN) are thirteen slots, each with a shuttle containing the name of a single colony. This device, during a vote, is the province of the Secretary of the Congress.

At rise, the Chamber is empty save for its aging custodian, Andrew McNair, who is preparing the room for the day's session with the help of a Leather Apron, a working man. The wall calendar now reads: "JUNE 7." Then, as McNair sets out quill pens and fills the several inkwells from a large jar, Georgia's Dr. Lyman Hall, fifty-five, enters and looks around, finally clearing his throat. McNair looks up.

MCNAIR:
Yes?

HALL:
I'm Dr. Lyman Hall, a new delegate from Georgia.

MCNAIR:
I'm Andrew McNair, Congressional Custodian. [*He goes back to work.*] If you'll be wantin' anything at all just holler out, "McNair!" as you'll hear the others do, and there won't be too long to wait.

HALL, *looking around:*
Where does the Georgia delegation belong?

MCNAIR:
Oh, they mill about over in that corner—near the two Carolinas.

HALL, *checking his watch:*
> It's after ten. I was told the Congress convenes at
> ten.

MCNAIR:
> They'll be wanderin' in any time now, sir—with
> Old Grape 'n' Guts leadin' the pack.

HALL:
> Old *who?*

HOPKINS' VOICE, *offstage:*
> *McNair!!*

MCNAIR:
> Grape 'n' Guts.

> *Stephen Hopkins, a thin round-shouldered man of*
> *seventy, wearing a black suit, black Quaker hat, his*
> *gray hair at shoulder length, enters.*

HOPKINS:
> Fetch me a mug o' rum!

MCNAIR:
> Mr. Hopkins, you'll be pleased to meet Dr. Lyman
> Hall—

HOPKINS:
> I don't need a doctor, dammit—

MCNAIR:
> —new delegate from Georgia—

HOPKINS:
> Why didn't you say so? [*To Hall:*] I'm Stephen
> Hopkins, *old* delegate from Rhode Island. McNair!
> *Two* mugs o' rum!

HALL:
> I fear it's a little early in the day—

HOPKINS:
> Nonsense! It's a medicinal fact that rum gets a

man's heart started in the morning—I'm surprised
you didn't know it. And speaking as the oldest man
in the Congress—

MCNAIR:
Ben Franklin's older by almost a year—

HOPKINS:
Rum!!

McNair scurries off.

Tell me, Dr. Hall, where does Georgia stand on the
question of independence?

*Edward Rutledge, a young, handsome, dandified
aristocrat of twenty-six, has entered.*

RUTLEDGE:
With South Carolina, of course.

HOPKINS, *laughing:*
Good morning, Neddy. Shake the hand of Dr. Lyman Hall from Georgia. Doctor, this here is Edward Rutledge from whichever Carolina he says
he's from—God knows I can't keep 'em straight.

RUTLEDGE:
A pleasure, Dr. Hall.

HALL:
Your servant, Mr. Rutledge.

HOPKINS:
You've met the long and short of it now, Doctor.
Neddy here is only twenty-six; he's the *youngest*
of us—

RUTLEDGE:
Except for Ben Franklin—

HOPKINS:
McNair!!

*McNair has returned and now stands at Hopkins'
elbow.*

MCNAIR:
Your rum.

HOPKINS:
Where'd y'go for it, man—Jamaica?

Rutledge and Hall walk away.

RUTLEDGE:
Where *does* Georgia stand on independence at the
present time, Dr. Hall?

HALL:
I am here without instructions, able to vote my own
personal convictions.

RUTLEDGE:
And they are—?

HALL, *a pause; he examines him:*
Personal.

RUTLEDGE:
Dr. Hall, the Deep South speaks with one voice. It
is traditional—even more, it is historical.

*They regard one another for a moment. Then the
Delaware delegation enters: Caesar Rodney, forty-
eight, thin and pale, wears a green scarf tied
around his face, covering some infirmity; George
Read, forty-three, small and round, speaks with a
high voice; and Colonel Thomas McKean, forty-
two, tall and florid, has a booming voice decorated
with a Scottish brogue. As always, the three are
arguing.*

Enter Delaware—*tria juncta in uno!*

McKEAN:

Speak plain, Rutledge, y'know I can't follow none
o' y'r damn French!

RUTLEDGE:

Latin, Colonel McKean—a tribute to the eternal
peace and harmony of the Delaware delegation.

McKEAN:

What're .y'sayin', man? Y'know perfectly well
neither Rodney nor I can stand this little wart!
[*He indicates Read.*]

RUTLEDGE:

Gentlemen, gentlemen, this is Dr. Lyman Hall of
Georgia—Caesar Rodney, George Read, and Colonel Thomas McKean.
*Hall shakes hands with each in turn and they ex-
change greetings.*

RODNEY:

Where do you stand on independence, sir?

HALL—*a look to Rutledge:*

With South Carolina, it seems.

RUTLEDGE:

I leave the doctor in your excellent company,
gentlemen.
*Smiling, he bows and walks away, joining another
group.*
*Slowly the Chamber has begun to fill with Con-
gressmen: Lewis Morris and Robert Livingston of
New York; Roger Sherman of Connecticut; Joseph
Hewes of North Coralina; the portly Samuel Chase
of Maryland; Josiah Bartlett of New Hampshire;
others; and last to enter, unnoticed, Thomas Jefferson of Virginia, thirty-three, six feet three, with
copper-colored hair, carrying several books.*

RODNEY, *drawing Hall aside:*

Tell me, sir, would you be a doctor of medicine or theology?

HALL:

Both, Mr. Rodney. Which one can be of service?

RODNEY, *good-naturedly:*

By all means the physician first! Then we shall see about the other.

HALL, *smiling:*

I'll call at your convenience, sir.

They are joined by two members of the Pennsylvania delegation: John Dickinson, forty-four, a thin, hawkish man, not without elegance, and James Wilson, thirty-three, a bespectacled, cautious little sycophant.

DICKINSON, *pleasantly:*

I trust, Caesar, when you're through converting the poor fellow to independency that you'll give the opposition a fair crack at him.

RODNEY:

You're too late, John; once I get 'em they're got. Dr. Lyman Hall of Georgia—Mr. John Dickinson of Pennsylvania:

DICKINSON:

An honor, sir.

HALL:

Your servant.

WILSON, *waiting:*

Ahem.

RODNEY:

Ah, Judge Wilson, forgive me—but how can anyone see you if you insist on standing in Mr. Dickin-

son's shadow? [*To Hall*] James Wilson, also of
Pennsylvania.

WILSON:
Sir.

HALL:
An honor, sir.

*Franklin enters, limping on a cane, one foot ban-
daged.*

FRANKLIN:
Will you get out of my way, please? Good morning,
all!

HALL, *recognizing him:*
Good Lord, do you have the honor to be Dr.
Franklin?

FRANKLIN:
Yes, I have that honor—unfortunately the gout ac-
companies the honor.

HOPKINS:
Been living too high again, eh, Pappy?

FRANKLIN:
Stephen, I only wish King George felt like my big
toe—all over!

HOPKINS:
McNair!! Fetch a pillow—and two more mugs of
rum!

*Now John enters the Chamber and looks around,
searching for someone.*
   *It is now evident that the colors and styles of the
various costumes change gradually from colony to
colony—from the fancy greens and golds of the
Deep South to the somber blacks of New England.*

FRANKLIN:

Good morning, John!

JOHN, *joining him:*

Well, Franklin? Where's that idiot Lee? Has he returned yet? I don't see him.

FRANKLIN:

Softly, John—your voice is hurting my foot.

JOHN:

One more day, Franklin—that's how long I'll remain silent, and not a minute longer! That strutting popinjay was so damned sure of himself. He's had time to bring back a *dozen* proposals by now!

Dickinson turns to Wilson and addresses him in a loud voice, for all to hear.

DICKINSON:

Tell me, James, how do you explain the strange, monumental quietude that Congress has been treated to these past thirty days?

Everyone, including John, has turned to listen.

Has the ill wind of independence finally blown itself out?

WILSON:

If you ask me—

DICKINSON:

For myself, I must confess that a month free from New England noise is more therapeutic than a month in the country! Don't you agree, James?

WILSON:

Well, I—

DICKINSON, *turning:*

Mr. Adams, pray look for your voice, sir! It cannot be far and God knows we need the entertainment in this Congress!

Laughter from his fellow conservatives. Everyone turns to Adams, who is trembling with rage.

FRANKLIN:

Congratulations, John, you've just made your greatest contribution to independence—you kept your flap shut!

JOHN:

One more day . . . !

John Hancock, forty, takes his place at the President's desk; he is followed by Charles Thomson, forty-seven, the pedantic Secretary to the Congress. Hancock pounds his gavel.

HANCOCK:

Gentlemen, the usual morning festivities concluded, I will now call the Congress to order. [*Gavel:*] Mr. Thomson.

THOMSON, *rising and ringing a bell:*

The Second Continental Congress, meeting in the city of Philadelphia, is now in session, seventh June, seventeen seventy-six, the three hundred eightieth meeting.

MCNAIR:

Sweet Jesus!

THOMSON:

The Honorable John Hancock of Massachusetts Bay, President. [*He rings the bells and sits.*]

HANCOCK:

Thank you, Mr. Thomson. [*He swats a fly.*] Mr. McNair, the stores of rum and other drinking spirits are hereby closed to the colony of Rhode Island for a period of three days.

MCNAIR:

Yes, sir.

HOPKINS:

John, y'can't do that!

HANCOCK:

Sit down, Mr. Hopkins. You've abused the privilege. The Chair takes this opportunity to welcome Dr. Lyman Hall of Georgia to this Congress and hopes he will make the best of it. My God, it's hot! The Secretary will read the roll.

THOMSON:

All members present with the following exceptions: Mr. Charles Carroll of Maryland; Mr. Samuel Adams of Massachusetts; Mr. Button Gwinnett of Georgia; Mr. George Wythe and Mr. Richard Henry Lee of Virginia; and the entire delegation of New Jersey.

HANCOCK:

I'm concerned over the continued absence of one-thirteenth of this Congress. Where *is* New Jersey?

DICKINSON:

Somewhere between New York and Pennsylvania.

HANCOCK:

Thank you very much. Dr. Franklin, have *you* heard anything? Your son resides there.

FRANKLIN:

Son, sir? What son?

HANCOCK—*sorry he brought it up:*

The Royal Governor of New Jersey, sir.

FRANKLIN:

As that title might suggest, sir, we are not in touch at the present time.

HANCOCK:

Yes. Very well—uh—the weather report—Mr. Jefferson of Virginia.

No reaction; Jefferson is reading a book.

Mr. Jefferson!

JEFFERSON, *jumping to his feet:*
Present, sir!

HANCOCK:
May we hear about the weather, as if it weren't speaking for itself.

JEFFERSON, *going to several gauges at the window:*
Eighty-seven degrees of temperature, thirty-point-aught-six inches of mercury, wind from the southwest for the rest of the day, and tonight—[*he turns*] —tonight I'm leaving for home.

HANCOCK:
On business?

JEFFERSON:
Family business.

HOPKINS:
Give her a good one for me, young feller!

JEFFERSON, *smiling:*
Yes, sir, I will.

A uniformed courier, dusty from his long ride, enters and approaches Thomson, removing a communiqué from his pouch. He tosses it onto the Secretary's desk and leaves wearily.

THOMSON, *ringing his bell:*
From the Commander, Army of the United Colonies; in New York, dispatch number one thousand, one hundred and thirty-seven—

McNAIR:
Sweet Jesus!

THOMSON, *reading:*
"To the Honorable Congress, John Hancock, Presi-

dent. Dear Sir: It is with grave apprehension that I have learned this day of the sailing, from Halifax, Nova Scotia, of a considerable force of British troops in the company of foreign mercenaries and under the command of General Sir William Howe. There can be no doubt that their destination is New York, for to take and hold this city and the Hudson Valley beyond would serve to separate New England from the other colonies permitting both sections to be crushed in turn. Sadly, I see no way of stopping them at the present time as my army is absolutely falling apart, my military chest is totally exhausted, my Commissary General has strained his credit to the last, my Quartermaster has no food, no arms, no ammunition, and my troops are in a state of near mutiny! I pray God some relief arrives before the armada but fear it will not. Y'r ob'd't—"

Drum roll.

"G. Washington."

During the brief silence that follows, Thomson shrugs and files the dispatch.

McKEAN:
Mr. President!

HANCOCK, *wearily; he knows what's coming:*
Colonel McKean.

McKEAN:
Surely we've managed to promote the *gloomiest* man on this continent to the head of our troops. Those dispatches are the most depressing accumulation of disaster, doom, and despair in the entire annals of military history! And furthermore—

HANCOCK, *pounding his gavel:*
Please, Colonel McKean—it's too hot.

MCKEAN:

    Oh. Yes. I suppose so.

HANCOCK:

    General Washington will continue wording his dis-
    patches as he sees fit, and I'm sure we all pray that
    he finds happier thoughts to convey in the near
    —[*swats a fly*]—future. Mr. Thomson, are there
    any resolutions?

THOMSON:

    Dr. Josiah Bartlett of New Hampshire.

BARTLETT, *rising and reading:*

    "Resolved: that for the duration of the present
    hostilities the Congress discourage every type of
    extravagance and dissipation, elaborate funerals
    and other expensive diversions, especially all horse-
    racing—"

    *He is shouted down by the entire Congress. Then
    the door bursts open and Lee sweeps in.*

LEE:

    Benjy, I'm back—I'm back, Johnny! [*He lets out
    a Southern war whoop.*]

    *In a flash, John, Jefferson, McKean, and even the
    hobbling Franklin crowd around him.*

MCKEAN:

    Richard, we're pleased t'see y'!

FRANKLIN:

    What news, Dickie boy, what news?

JOHN:

    Lee! Is it done?

LEE:

    First things first. [*Looking around:*] Tom—where's
    Tom? [*Turning and seeing Jefferson:*] Tom! Your

little bride wants to know: "When's he coming home?"

JEFFERSON:

I leave tonight!

JOHN, *grabbing Lee's shoulders:*
Never mind that—*is it done?*

LEE:

Done? [*A pause.*] Why, certain-*Lee!*

Cheers from those for independence.

Mr. President, I have returned from Virginia with the followin' resolution. [*He produces a paper and reads.*] "Resolved: that these united colonies are (and of a right ought to be) free and independent states, that they are absolved from all allegiance to the British Crown, and that all political connection between them and the state of Great Britain is (and ought to be) totally dissolved!"

JOHN:

Mr. President, I second the proposal!

A silence; then Hancock swats a fly.

HANCOCK:

The resolution has been proposed and seconded. The Chair will now entertain debate.

DICKINSON, *rising, assuming weariness:*
Mr. President, Pennsylvania moves, as always, that the question of independence be postponed—indefinitely.

WILSON:

I second the motion!

HANCOCK:

Judge Wilson, in your eagerness to be loved you seem to have forgotten that Pennsylvania cannot second its own motion.

READ:
    Delaware seconds.

McKEAN:
    You would, y'little weasel!

HANCOCK:
    The motion to postpone has been moved and sec-
    onded. Mr. Thomson.

    *Thomson goes to the tally board. As each colony
    votes, he announces it and McNair, in turn,
    mechanically records it on the board.*

    *Hopkins, during his preparation, rises and leaves
    the Chamber.*

THOMSON:
    On the motion to postpone indefinitely the resolu-
    tion of independency or proceed with the debate,
    all those in favor of debate say "Yea," all those for
    postponement say "Nay." [*Intoning:*] New Hamp-
    shire—

BARTLETT:
    New Hampshire favors debate and says Yea.

THOMSON:
    New Hampshire says Yea. Massachusetts—

JOHN:
    Massachusetts, having borne the brunt of the King's
    tyranny—

THOSE AGAINST:
    Shame!! Shame!!

THOSE FOR:
    Sit down, John!

JOHN:
    Yes, I said *tyranny!* Massachusetts now and for all
    time says *Yea!*

THOMSON, *flatly:*

> Massachusetts says Yea. Rhode Island—Mr. Hop-
> kins? Where's Rhode Island?

MCNAIR:

> Rhode Island is out visitin' the "necessary."

HANCOCK:

> After what Rhode Island's consumed, I can't say
> I'm surprised. We'll come back to him, Mr. Thom-
> son.

THOMSON:

> Rhode Island passes.

> *Laughter; Thomson looks around, not understand-*
> *ing, then proceeds.*

> Connecticut—

SHERMAN—*he holds, as he will throughout the entire*
play, a shallow bowl of coffee; he is never without
it:

> While Connecticut has, till now, been against this
> proposal, our legislature has instructed me that, in
> the event it is introduced by any colony *outside* of
> New England, Connecticut could not any longer
> withhold its support. Connecticut says Yea.

> *Franklin and John exchange satisfied looks.*

THOMSON:

> Connecticut says Yea. New York—

MORRIS:

> Mr. Secretary, New York abstains—courteously.

THOMSON:

> New York abstains—

MORRIS:

> —courteously.

THOMSON:
   New Jersey—

HANCOCK:
   Absent, Mr. Secretary.

THOMSON:
   New Jersey is absent. Pennsylvania—

DICKINSON:
   Pennsylvania, for the twenty-fourth time, says
   Nay.

THOMSON:
   Pennsylvania says Nay. Delaware—

RODNEY:
   Delaware, as ever for independence, says Yea.

THOMSON:
   Delaware says Yea. Mary-land—

CHASE:
   Mary-land would welcome independence if it were
   given but is highly skeptical that it can be taken.
   Mary-land says Nay.

THOMSON:
   Mary-land says Nay. Virginia—

LEE:
   Virginia, the First Colony, says Yea!

THOMSON:
   Virginia says Yea. North Carolina—

HEWES:
   North Carolina respectfully yields to *South* Carolina.

THOMSON:
   South Carolina—

RUTLEDGE:
   Mr. President, although we in South Carolina have

never seriously considered the question of independence, when a *gentleman* proposes it, attention
must be paid. However—we in the Deep South, un-
like our friends in New England, have no cause for
impatience at the present time. If, at some future
date, it becomes the wish of *all* our sister colonies
to effect a separation, we will not stand in the way.
But for the time bein', South Carolina will wait—
and watch. The vote is Nay.

THOMSON:
South Carolina says Nay.

HEWES, *jumping up:*
North Carolina—

THOMSON:
—says Nay. Yes, Mr. Hewes, I know. Georgia—

*Hall rises, looks around, but says nothing, obvi-
ously in great uncertainty.*

Georgia—

HALL:
Mr. Secretary—[*His eyes meet Rutledge's, then
quickly look away.*] Georgia seems to be split right
down the middle on this issue. The people are
against it—and I'm for it.

Understanding laughter.

But I'm afraid I'm not yet certain whether representing the people means relying on their judgment
or on my own. So in all fairness, until I can figure
it out, I'd better lean a little toward their side.
Georgia says Nay.

THOMSON:
Georgia says Nay. [*He checks the board.*] Rhode
Island. [*Calling off:*] *Second call—Rhode Island!*

HOPKINS, *offstage:*

> I'm comin'! I'm comin'! [*Entering:*] Hold y'r damn horses!

THOMSON:

> We're waiting on *you,* Mr. Hopkins.

HOPKINS:

> It won't kill you. You'd think the Congress would have its own pisser! All right, where does she stand?

THOMSON:

> Five for debate, five for postponement, one abstention, and one absence.

HOPKINS:

> So it's up to me, is it? Well, I'll tell y'—in all my years I never heard, seen, nor smelled an issue that was so dangerous it couldn't be talked about. Hell yes, I'm for debatin' anything—Rhode Island says Yea!

> *Cheers from those for, including another war whoop from Lee, as they crowd around Hopkins.*

HANCOCK:

> McNair, get Mr. Hopkins a rum!

MCNAIR:

> But you said—

HANCOCK:

> Get him the whole damn barrel if he wants!

MCNAIR:

> Yes, sir!

HANCOCK:

> The Chair now declares this Congress a committee-of-the-whole for the purpose of debating Virginia's resolution of independence. Mr. Dickinson.

DICKINSON:

Well, now. You've got your way at last, Mr. Adams—the matter may now be discussed. I confess I'm almost relieved. There's a question I've been fairly itching to ask you: Why?

JOHN:

Why what, Mr. Dickinson?

DICKINSON:

Why independence, Mr. Adams?

JOHN:

For the obvious reason that our continued association with Great Britain has grown intolerable.

DICKINSON:

To whom, Mr. Adams? To you? Then I suggest you sever your ties immediately. But please be kind enough to leave the rest of us where we are. Personally, I have no objections at all to being part of the greatest empire on earth, to enjoying its protection and sharing its benefits—

JOHN:

Benefits? What benefits? Crippling taxes? Cruel repressions? Abolished rights?

DICKINSON:

Is that all England means to you, sir? Is that *all* the affection and pride you can muster for the nation that bore you—for the noblest, most civilized nation on the face of this planet? Would you have us forsake Hastings and Magna Carta, Strongbow and Lionhearted, Drake and Marlborough, Tudors, Stuarts, and Plantagenets? For what, sir? Tell me for what? For *you?*

He smiles, then turns.

Some men are patriots, like General Washington—some are anarchists, like Mr. Paine—some even are internationalists, like Dr. Franklin. But you, sir, you are merely an *a-gi-ta-tor*, disturbing the peace, creating disorder, endangering the public welfare—and for what? Your petty little personal complaints. Your taxes are too high. Well, sir, so are mine. Come, come, Mr. Adams, if you have grievances—and I'm sure you have—our present system must provide a gentler means of redressing them short of—[*suddenly his manner changes as he brings his fist down on the desk with a crash*] —revolution!! [*Wheeling to the Congress:*] That's what *he* wants—nothing less will satisfy him! Violence! Rebellion! *Treason!* Now, Mr. Adams, are these the acts of Englishmen?

JOHN:
Not Englishmen, Dickinson—Americans!

DICKINSON, *again pounding the desk:*
No, sir! *Englishmen!!*

FRANKLIN—*he's been asleep, his chin on his chest; now an eye opens:*

Please, Mr. Dickinson—but must you start banging? How is a man to sleep?

Laughter.

DICKINSON:
Forgive me, Dr. Franklin, but must you start speaking? How is a man to stay awake?

Laughter.

We'll promise to be quiet, sir. I'm sure everyone prefers that you remain asleep.

FRANKLIN:
If I'm to hear myself called an Englishman, sir, then I assure you I'd prefer I'd remained asleep.

DICKINSON:

What's so terrible about being called an Englishman? The English don't seem to mind.

FRANKLIN:

Nor would I, were I given the full rights of an Englishman. But to call me one *without* those rights is like calling an ox a bull—he's thankful for the honor but he'd much rather have restored what's rightfully his.

Laughter, Franklin laughing the longest.

DICKINSON, *finally:*

When did you first notice they were missing, sir?

Laughter.

Fortunately, Dr. Franklin, the people of these colonies maintain a higher regard for their mother country.

FRANKLIN:

Higher, certainly, than she feels for them. Never was such a valuable possession so stupidly and recklessly managed than this entire continent by the British Crown. Our industry discouraged, our resources pillaged—and, worst of all, our very character stifled. We've spawned a new race here—rougher, simpler, more violent, more enterprising, and less refined. We're a new nationality, Mr. Dickinson—we require a new nation.

DICKINSON:

That may be your opinion, Dr. Franklin, but as I said, the people feel quite differently.

JOHN:

What do you know about the people, Dickinson? You don't speak for the people: you represent only yourself. And that precious "status quo" you

keep imploring the people to preserve for *their*
own good is nothing more than the eternal preser-
vation of *your* own property!

DICKINSON:

Mr. Adams, you have an annoying talent for making such delightful words as "property" sound
quite distasteful. In Heaven's name, what's wrong
with property? Perhaps you've forgotten that many
of us first came to these shores in order to secure
rights to property—and that we hold *those* rights
no less dear than the rights you speak of.

JOHN:

So safe, so fat, so comfortable in Pennsylvania—

DICKINSON:

And what is this independence of yours except
the private grievance of Massachusetts? Why, even
your own cousin, so busy now with his seditious
activities in Boston that he has no time to attend
this Congress, is a fugitive with a price on his head!

HANCOCK:

Slowly, Mr. Dickinson. I remind you that the same
price that covers Sam Adams also covets me—
we are wanted together.

DICKINSON:

What did you expect? You both dress up like red
savages in order to commit piracy against one of
His Majesty's ships—an event so embarrassing to
your sister colonies that even your good friend Dr.
Franklin offered to pay for all that spilt tea from
his own pocket!

FRANKLIN:

I'm usually able to speak for myself, Mr. Dickinson.

SCENE 3 / 1776

DICKINSON:

Then tell me this: what good can come from this radicalism and civil disorder? Where can it lead except to chaos, mob rule, and anarchy? And why in God's name is it always *Boston* that breaks the King's peace? [*To the Congress:*] My dear Congress you must not adopt this evil measure. It is the work of the devil. Leave it where it belongs— in New England.

SHERMAN:

Brother Dickinson, New England his been fighting the devil for more than a hundred years.

DICKINSON:

And as of now, "Brother" Sherman, the devil has been winning hands down! [*Indicating John:*] Why, at this very moment he is sitting here in this Congress! Don't let him deceive you—this proposal is entirely his doing! It may bear Virginia's name, but it reeks of Adams, Adams, and more Adams! Look at him—ready to lead this continent down the fiery path of total destruction!

JOHN:

Good God! Why can't you acknowledge what already exists? It has been more than a year since Concord and Lexington. Dammit, man, we're at war right now!

DICKINSON:

You may be at war—you: Boston and John Adams—but you will never speak for Pennsylvania!

READ, *jumping up:*
Nor for Delaware!

RODNEY:

Mr. Read, you represent only one-third of Delaware!

READ:
> The sensible third, Mr. Rodney!

McKEAN:
> Sit down, y'little roach, or I'll knock y'down!

HANCOCK:
> Sit down, all three of you! *McNair!!* Do something about these damned flies!

HOPKINS:
> *McNair!!* Fetch me a rum!

HANCOCK:
> Get the flies first!

McNAIR:
> I've only got two hands!

HANCOCK, *mopping his brow:*
> Christ, it's hot! Please do go on, gentlemen; you're making the only breeze in Philadelphia.

RUTLEDGE:
> Mr. Adams, perhaps you could clear something up for *me:* after we have achieved independence, who do you propose would govern in South Carolina?

JOHN:
> The people, of course.

RUTLEDGE:
> Which people, sir? The people of South Carolina? Or the people of Massachusetts?

HOPKINS:
> Why don't you admit it, Neddy? You're against independence now, and you always will be.

McKEAN:
> Aye!

RUTLEDGE:

You refuse to understand us, gentlemen! We desire independence, yes—for South Carolina. That is our country. And as such we don't wish it to belong to anyone—not to England, and not to you.

JOHN:

We intend to be one nation, Rutledge.

RUTLEDGE:

A nation of sovereign states, Mr. Adams, united for our mutual protection, but separate for our individual pursuits. That is what we have understood it to be, and that is what we will support— as soon as *every*one supports it.

WILSON:

There you are, Mr. Adams, you must see that we need time to make certain who we are and where we stand in regard to one another—for if we do not determine the nature of the beast before we set it free, it will end by consuming us all.

JOHN:

For once in your life, Wilson—take a chance. I say the time is now! It may never come again!

HEWES:

Your clock is fast, Mr. Adams. I say we're not yet ripe for independence.

HOPKINS:

Not ripe? Hell, we're *rotting* for want of it!

CHASE:

Gentlemen, please. What in God's name is the infernal hurry? Why must this question be settled now?

RODNEY:

What's wrong with now, Mr. Chase?

CHASE:

General Washington is in the field. If he's defeated, as it now appears, we'll be inviting the hangman. But if, by some miracle, he should actually win, we can then declare anything we damn please!

HEWES:

The sentiments of North Carolina precisely.

JOHN:

Has it ever occurred to either of you that an army needs something to fight for in order *to* win—a cause, a purpose, a flag of its own?

CHASE:

Mr. Adams, how can a nation of only two million souls stand up to an empire of ten million? Think of it—*ten million!* How do we *compensate* for that shortage?

FRANKLIN:

It's simple, Mr. Chase—increase and multiply!

CHASE:

How's that?

JOHN:

We will more than compensate—with *spirit!* I tell you there's a spirit out there with the people that's sadly lacking in this Congress!

DICKINSON:

Yes, of course—now it's *spirit!* Why didn't I think of that? No army, no navy, no arms, no ammunition, no treasury, no friends—but, bless our soul, *spirit!* [*Turning:*] Mr. Lee, Mr. Hopkins, Mr. Rodney, Colonel McKean, Dr. Franklin, why have you joined this incendiary little man? This Boston radical, this *a-gi-ta-tor*, this demagogue—this *madman!*

JOHN:

> Are you calling me a madman, you—you—you—
> *fribble!!*

FRANKLIN:

> Easy, John!

JOHN:

> You and your Pennsylvania proprietors—you cool,
> considerate men! You keep to the rear of every
> issue so if we should go under you'll still remain
> afloat!

DICKINSON:

> Are you calling me a coward?

JOHN:

> Yes! *Coward!!*

DICKINSON:

> *Madman!!*

JOHN:

> *Landlord!!*

DICKINSON:

> *Lawyer!!*

> *The battle is joined. They begin whacking away at
> each other with their walking sticks. Congress is
> in an uproar.*

HOPKINS:

> Whack him, John!

FRANKLIN:

> Ho, Spartacus!

CONGRESS:

> Stop! Go! For shame! At Last! [*Et cetera.*]

> *Rodney now steps forward, between them, and
> pushes them apart.*

RODNEY:
Stop it! *Stop it!!* This is the Congress! Stop it, I say! The enemy is out there!

DICKINSON:
No, Mr. Rodney, the enemy is here!

RODNEY:
No, no, I say he's out there—England, *England,* closing in, cutting off our air—there's no time— no air—[*He is stricken.*] Thomas! [*He collapses into McKean's arms.*]

MCKEAN:
Caesar—*Caesar!!*

He looks around as the Congress falls silent and moves in.

Doctor Hall?

HALL, *kneeling beside Rodney and looking under the green scarf; his expression reflects what he finds:* Colonel McKean—

MCKEAN:
Aye, it's the cancer.

HALL:
He should go home.

RODNEY, *disgusted with himself:*
Yes, a man should die in his own bed. John—John Adams—

JOHN:
I'm here, Caesar.

RODNEY:
I leave you a divided Delaware. Forgive me.

MCKEAN:
I'll take y'home, Caesar. [*He lifts Rodney and*

turns to John.] I'll be back within the week. [*He carries Rodney out.*]

There is a moment of silence; then Rutledge steps forward.

RUTLEDGE:
Mr. President, South Carolina calls the question.

HANCOCK, *distracted:*
What's that, Mr. Rutledge?

RUTLEDGE, *walking to the tally board:*
I said, Mr. President, South Carolina desires to end the debate and—[*he moves the Delaware marker from the "Yea" to the "Nay" column*]— call the question of independence.

READ, *glowing:*
Delaware seconds!

Again, bedlam, as everyone understands what has happened.

CONGRESS:
No! Yes! You can't do that! Call the question! [*Et cetera.*]

HANCOCK, *pounding for order:*
Gentlemen, *please!* The question has been called and seconded. Mr. Secretary, you will record the vote.

JOHN, *to Franklin:*
Franklin, do something—*think!*

FRANKLIN:
I'm thinking, I'm thinking—but nothing's coming!

THOMSON:
All those in favor of the resolution on independence as proposed by the colony of Virginia signify by saying—

FRANKLIN:

> Mr. Secretary, would you read the resolution again? [*As everyone looks at him in surprise, he shrugs.*] I've forgotten it.

> *Annoyed, Thomson looks to Hancock, who nods; he sighs.*

THOMSON:

> "Resolved: That these United Colonies are (and of a right ought to be) free and independent—"

> *The Reverend John Witherspoon, a lean and as-cetic clergyman of fifty-four, enters.*

WITHERSPOON:

> I beg your pardon, I'm the Reverend John Wither-spoon, new delegate from New Jersey—?

> *As everyone moves in expectantly, he draws back, then seeks out the only familiar face.*

> Dr. Franklin, I regret I must be the bearer of un-happy tidings, but your son, the Royal Governor of New Jersey, is taken prisoner and has been moved under guard to the colony of Connecticut for safe-keeping.

FRANKLIN:

> Is he unharmed, sir?

WITHERSPOON:

> When last I heard, he was, yes, sir.

FRANKLIN:

> Then why the long face? I hear Connecticut is an excellent location. Why'd they arrest the little bastard?

WITHERSPOON, *rattled:*

> Our—uh—New Jersey legislature has recalled the old delegation to this Congress and has sent a new one.

JOHN:

Quickly, man—where do y'stand on independence?

WITHERSPOON:

Oh, haven't I made that clear? I s'pose I haven't.
But that was the reason for the change—we've
been instructed to vote *for* independence.

JOHN, *quickly:*

Mr. President! [*He goes to the tally board.*] Massachusetts is now ready for the vote on independence—[*he records New Jersey under the "Yes"
column*]—and reminds the Chair of its privilege
to decide all votes that are deadlocked!

HANCOCK:

I won't forget, Mr. Adams. The Chair would like
to welcome the Reverend Witherspoon and appoint
him Congressional Chaplain if he will accept the
post.

WITHERSPOON:

With much pleasure, sir.

HANCOCK:

Very well. Mr. Thomson, you may now—[*he swats
a fly*]—proceed with the vote on independence.

THOMSON:

All in favor of the resolution on independence as
proposed by the colony of Virginia signify by saying—

DICKINSON, *jumping up:*

Mr. President, Pennsylvania moves that any vote
in favor of independence must be unanimous!

JOHN:

What?

WILSON:

I second the motion!

HANCOCK, *admonishing:*
Judge Wilson—

WILSON, *chagrined:*
Oh my God.

READ:
Delaware seconds, Mr. President.

JOHN:
No vote's ever had to be unanimous, Dickinson, and you know it!

DICKINSON:
Yes, but this one must be.

JOHN:
On what grounds?

DICKINSON:
That no colony be torn from its mother country without its own consent.

RUTLEDGE:
Hear, hear!

JOHN:
But it'll never be unanimous, dammit!

DICKINSON:
If you say so, Mr. Adams.

THOMSON:
It has been moved and seconded that the vote on independence must be unanimous in order to carry. All those in favor signify by saying "Yea".

Dickinson, Chase, Read, Rutledge, Hewes, and Hall say "Yea."

Six colonies say "Yea." All those opposed signify by saying "Nay."

John, Bartlett, Hopkins, Sherman, Lee, and Witherspoon say "Nay."

Six colonies say "Nay."

MORRIS:

Mr. Secretary, New York abstains—courteously.

HANCOCK:

Mr. Morris, why does New York constantly abstain? Why doesn't New York simply stay in New York? Very well, the vote is tied. [*He covers his eyes for a moment.*] The principles of independence have no greater advocate in Congress than its President—and that is why I must join those who vote *for* unanimity.

JOHN—*as the Congress reacts, stunned, he jumps up, horrified:* Good God! What're y'doing, John? You've sunk us!

HANCOCK:

Hear me out. Don't you see that any colony who opposes independence will be forced to fight on the side of England—that we'll be setting brother against brother, that our new nation will carry as its emblem the mark of Cain? I can see no other way. Either we walk together or together we must stay where we are.

A silence.

Very well. Proceed, Mr. Thomson.

THOMSON:

A unanimous vote being necessary to carry, if any be opposed to the resolution on independence as proposed by the colony of Virginia, signify by saying—

JOHN:

Mr. President!!

THOMSON:

  For heaven's sake, let me get through it *once!*

JOHN:

  Mr. President, I move for a postponement!

DICKINSON:

  Ha! I wish you the same luck *I* had with it!

FRANKLIN:

  Mr. Adams is right, we need a postponement!

DICKINSON:

  On what grounds?

FRANKLIN, *to John:*

  On what grounds?

JOHN:

  Mr. President, how can this Congress vote on
  independence without—uh—a written declaration
  of some sort defining it?

HANCOCK:

  What sort of declaration?

JOHN:

  Well, you know—uh—listing all the reasons for
  the separation and—uh—our goals and aims and
  so on and so forth, ditto, ditto, et cetera, et cetera.

HANCOCK, *not getting it:*

  We know those, don't we?

JOHN:

  Well, good God, yes, *we* know them, but what
  about the rest of the world? Certainly we require
  the aid of a powerful nation like France or Spain,
  and such a declaration would be consistent with
  European delicacy.

CHASE:

  Come, now, Mr. Adams, you'll have to do better

than that! Answer straight—what would be its purpose?

A pause; for once John is at a loss for words.

JOHN:

Yes, well—

JEFFERSON, *rising and speaking deliberately:*

To place before mankind the common sense of the subject, in terms so plain and firm as to command their assent.

Winking at John, he sits. A moment of surprise; then Dickinson laughs.

DICKINSON:

Mr. Jefferson, are you seriously suggesting that we publish a paper declaring to all the world that an illegal rebellion is, in reality, a legal one?

FRANKLIN:

Why, Mr. Dickinson, I'm surprised at you! You should know that rebellion is *always* legal in the first person—such as "our" rebellion. It is only in the third person—"their" rebellion—that it is *il*legal.

Laughter.

Mr. President, I second the motion to postpone the vote on independence for a period of time sufficient for the writing of a declaration.

HANCOCK:

It has been moved and seconded. Mr. Secretary—

THOMSON:

All those in favor of the motion to postpone signify by saying "Yea."

Adams, Bartlett, Hopkins, Sherman, Witherspoon, and Lee say "Yea."

Six colonies say "Yea." Against?

Dickinson, Chase, Read, Rutledge, Hewes, and Hall say "Nay."

Six colonies say "Nay."

MORRIS:

Mr. Secretary, New York abstains—courteously.

HANCOCK, *threatening him with his fly-swatter, then restraining himself:*

Mr. Morris! What in hell goes on in New York?

MORRIS:

I'm sorry, Mr. President, but the simple fact is that our legislature has never sent up explicit instructions on anything.

HANCOCK:

Never? That's impossible!

MORRIS:

Have you ever been present at a meeting of the New York legislature? They speak very fast and very loud and nobody pays any attention to anybody else, with the result that nothing ever gets done. I beg the Congress' pardon.

HANCOCK:

My sympathies, Mr. Morris. The vote again being tied, the Chair decides in favor of the postponement. [*His gavel.*] So ruled. A committee will now be formed to manage the declaration, said document to be written, debated, and approved by the beginning of July, three weeks hence, at which time Virginia's resolution on independence will finally be voted. Is that clear? [*Meeting general agreement:*] Very well. Will the following gentlemen serve on the Declaration Committee. Dr. Franklin,

Mr. John Adams, Mr. Sherman, Mr. Livingston, and, of course, Mr. Lee.

LEE:

Excuse me, but I must be returnin' to the sovereign country of Virginia as I have been asked to serve as governor. Therefore I must decline—respectful-*Lee!*

HANCOCK:

Very well, Mr. Lee, you're excused. I suppose we could leave it a four-man committee.

JOHN:

Just a moment. This business needs a Virginian. Therefore, I propose a replacement—Mr. Thomas Jefferson!

JEFFERSON:

No, Mr. Adams, *no!*

HANCOCK:

Very well, Mr. Adams, Mr. Jefferson will serve.

JEFFERSON:

I'm going home too—to my wife!

JOHN:

Move to adjourn!

JEFFERSON:

No, wait—

FRANKLIN:

Second!!

JEFFERSON:

It's been six months since I've seen her!

HANCOCK:

Moved and seconded—any objections?

JEFFERSON:

Yes! I have objections!

HANCOCK, *gaveling:*
> So ruled, Congress stands adjourned!

JEFFERSON, *on deaf ears:*
> I need to see my wife, I tell you!

> *Congress rises and goes as John, Franklin, Sherman and Livingston move downstage, with Jefferson following, still protesting.*

> *Music begins.*

JOHN:
> All right, gentlemen! Let's get on with it. Which of us is going to write our declaration on independence?

FRANKLIN, *singing:*
> Mr. Adams, I say you should write it,
> To your legal mind and brilliance we defer.

JOHN:
> Is that so!
> Well, if I'm the one to do it,
> They'll run their quill pens through it.
> I'm obnoxious and disliked, you know that, sir!

FRANKLIN, *speaking:*
> Yes, I know.

JOHN:
> Then I say you should write it, Franklin, yes, you!

FRANKLIN, *singing:*
> Hell, no!

JOHN:
> Yes, you, Dr. Franklin, you!

FRANKLIN:
> But—

JOHN:
> You!

FRANKLIN:
>But—

JOHN:
>You!

FRANKLIN:
>But—
>Mr. Adams!
>But—Mr. Adams!
>The things I write
>Are only light extemporanea.
>I won't put politics on paper.
>It's a mania.
>So, I refuse to use the pen—in Pennsylvania!

A Glee Club is formed by Sherman, Livingston, and Franklin.

GLEE CLUB:
>Pennsylvania!
>Pennsylvania!
>Refuse
>To use . . . the pen!

John begins to pace, thinking.

JOHN:
>Mr. Sherman, I say you should write it.
>You are never "controversial," as it were.

SHERMAN, *speaking:*
>That is true.

JOHN, *singing:*
>Whereas, if I'm the one to do it
>They'll run their quill pens through it.
>I'm obnoxious and disliked, you know that, sir.

SHERMAN, *speaking:*
>Yes, I do.

JOHN, *singing:*
> Then you should write it, Roger, you.

SHERMAN, *speaking:*
> Good heavens, no!

JOHN, *singing:*
> Yes, you, Roger Sherman, you!

SHERMAN:
> But—

JOHN:
> You!

SHERMAN:
> But—

JOHN:
> You!

SHERMAN:
> But—
> Mr. Adams!
> But—Mr. Adams!
> I cannot write with any style
> Or proper etiquette.
> I don't know a preposition
> From a predicate.
> I am just a simple cobbler
> From Connecticut!

GLEE CLUB:
> Connecticut!
> Connecticut!
> A simple cobbler . . . he!

> *John resumes his pacing.*

JOHN:
> Mr. Livingston, maybe you should write it.
> You have many friends, and you're a diplomat.

FRANKLIN, *speaking:*
> Oh, that word!

JOHN, *singing:*
> Whereas, if I'm the one to do it,
> They'll run their quill pens through it.

GLEE CLUB:
> He's obnoxious and disliked, did you know that?

LIVINGSTON, *speaking:*
> I hadn't heard—

JOHN, *singing:*
> Then I say you should write it, Robert! Yes, you!

LIVINGSTON, *speaking:*
> Not me, Johnny—

JOHN, *singing:*
> Yes! You, Robert Livingston—you!

LIVINGSTON:
> But—

JOHN:
> You!

LIVINGSTON:
> But—

JOHN:
> You!

LIVINGSTON:
> But—
> Mr. Adams!
> *Dear* Mr. Adams!
> I've been presented with a new son
> By the noble stork,
> So I am going home to celebrate
> And pop a cork
> With all the Livingstons together,
> Back in old New York!

GLEE CLUB:
>   New York!
>   New York!
>   Livingston's . . .
>   Going to pop . . . a cork!

Slowly, all eyes turn to Jefferson.

JEFFERSON:
>   Mr. Adams!
>   Leave me Alone!!!

The Glee Club sings a "La-la" theme, under.

JOHN, *speaking firmly:*
>   Mr. Jefferson—

JEFFERSON, *speaking:*
>   Mr. Adams, I beg you! I've not seen my wife these
>   six months!

JOHN, *quoting:*
>   ". . . and we solemnly declare we will preserve our
>   liberties, being with one mind resolved to die free
>   men—rather than to live slaves!"

The Glee Club stops to listen.

Thomas Jefferson, on the "Necessity of Taking Up
Arms," seventeen seventy-five, magnificent! You
write ten times better than any man in the Congress—including me! For a man of only thirty-three
years you possess a happy talent for composition
and a remarkable felicity of expression. Now! Will
you be a patriot? Or a lover?

JEFFERSON:
>   A lover!

JOHN:
>   No!

JEFFERSON, *singing:*
> But I burn, Mr. A.!

JOHN:
> So do I, Mr. J.!
>
> *Everything stops.*

JEFFERSON, *speaking:*
> You?

SHERMAN:
> You do?

FRANKLIN:
> John!

LIVINGSTON:
> Who'd 'a' thought it?

JOHN, *singing:*
> Mr. Jefferson,
> Dear Mr. Jefferson,
> I'm only forty-one,
> I still have my virility!
> And I can romp through Cupid's grove
> With great agility!
> But life is more than
> Sexual combustibility!

GLEE CLUB:
> Bust-a-bility!
> Bust-a-bility!
> Com-bust-a-bil-i—

JOHN, *shouting:*
> Quiet!
>
> *He sings:*
>
> Now, you'll write it, Mr. J.!

JEFFERSON, *six feet three:*
> Who will make me, Mr. A.?

JOHN, *five feet eight:*
    I!

JEFFERSON:
    You?

JOHN:
    Yes!

JEFFERSON:
    How?

JOHN, *speaking:*
    By—by physical force if necessary! It's your duty
    —*your duty, dammit!!*

JEFFERSON, *singing:*
    Mr. Adams!
    Damn you, Mr. Adams!
    You're obnoxious and disliked,
    That cannot be denied.

    This is agreed to by all.

    Once again you stand between me
    And my lovely bride!

GLEE CLUB:
    Lovely bride!

JEFFERSON:
    Oh, Mr. Adams, you are driving me . . . to
    Homicide!!

GLEE CLUB:
    Homicide!
    Homicide!

JOHN, *roaring:*
    Quiet!! [*He is furious.*] The choice is yours, Mr.
    Jefferson! [*He thrusts a large quill pen into Jeffer-
    son's hand; evenly:*] Do—as—you—like—with—
    it.

GLEE CLUB, *gleefully:*
>We may see mur-der yet!!

John goes, followed by the others.
>*Jefferson, alone, studies the pen for a moment, then turns and heads for his lodgings, still regarding the pen as he goes.*

SCENE 4

Jefferson's room, above High Street. It is spare and unaffected, like the man, with a desk, a cupboard, a chair, a couch, and a music stand; a violin sits on the desk.

Jefferson mounts the steps and enters his apartment. He takes another look at the pen and throws it onto the desk angrily.

JEFFERSON:

Damn the man! [*He removes his coat; then he catches sight of the pen again.*] GOD damn the man! [*Then, resigned, he sits at the desk and writes a few words. Suddenly he crumples the page and throws it on the floor. He writes some more; but again he crumples the paper and throws it on the floor. Now, merely thinking some unacceptable words, he crumples still another sheet, this one blank. Discouraged, he sits back, picks up his violin to play.*]

Meanwhile, John and Franklin have appeared outside and now enter. Franklin heads for the couch and stretches out, closing his eyes.

JOHN:

Jefferson, are y'finished?

There is no answer.

You've had a whole week, man. Is it done? Can I see it?

Jefferson points to all the crumpled paper on the floor. John picks one at random and, flattening it out, reads it.

JOHN:

> "There comes a time in the lives of men when it
> becomes necessary to advance from that subordina-
> tion in which they have hitherto remained—" this
> is terrible. [*Looking up.*] Where's the rest of it?

> *Again Jefferson points to the floor.*

> Do you mean to say it's *not* finished?

JEFFERSON:

> No, sir—I mean to say it's not begun.

JOHN:

> Good God! A whole week! The entire earth was
> created in a week!

JEFFERSON, *fed up, turning to John:*

> Some day you must tell me how you did it.

JOHN:

> Disgusting! Look at him, Franklin—Virginia's
> most famous lover—

JEFFERSON:

> Virginia abstains.

JOHN:

> Cheer up, Jefferson, get out of the dumps. It'll
> come out right, I promise you. Now get back to
> work. Franklin, tell him to get to work.

JEFFERSON:

> He's asleep.

> *Outside, a cloaked woman appears. She stops,
> looks around, then sees the door and enters. It is
> Martha, Jefferson's wife, a lovely girl of twenty-
> seven.*

FRANKLIN, *sitting bolt upright on the couch:*

> View-hal-*loo*, and whose-little-girl are you?

*But Jefferson and Martha are suddenly oblivious to
everything but each other as they meet and em-
brace. They kiss, and kiss, and will continue kissing
throughout the remainder of the scene.*

John, who is she?

JOHN:
  His wife—[*he studies them*]—I hope.

FRANKLIN, *his eyes never leaving them:*
  What makes y'think so?

JOHN:
  Because I sent for her.

FRANKLIN:
  Y'*what?*

JOHN:
  It simply occurred to me that the sooner his problem was solved, the sooner *our* problem was solved.

FRANKLIN:
  Good thinking, John, good thinking!

JOHN, *stepping forward:*
  Madame, may I present myself? John Adams.

  No reaction.

  Adams—*John Adams!*

  Nothing.

  And Dr. Franklin.

  Nothing.

  Inventor of the stove!!

  No luck.

  Jefferson, would you kindly present me to your
  wife?

  No reaction.

  She *is* your wife, isn't she?

FRANKLIN:

> Of course she is—look how they fit! [*Starting for the door:*] Come along, John, come along.

JOHN:

> Come along where? There's work to be done!

FRANKLIN, *with a look back over his shoulder:*

> Heh! Obviously!

> *Outside, on the street.*

JOHN:

> Good God! Y'mean they— They're going to— [*He stops.*] In the middle of the *afternoon?*

FRANKLIN:

> Not everybody's from Boston, John. [*He takes John's arm and leads him aside. John keeps looking back, unable to get over it.*]

JOHN:

> Incredible.

FRANKLIN:

> Well—good night, John.

JOHN:

> Have y'eaten, Franklin?

FRANKLIN:

> Not yet, but—

JOHN:

> I hear the turkey's fresh at the Bunch o' Grapes.

FRANKLIN:

> I have a rendezvous, John.

JOHN:

> Oh.

FRANKLIN:

> I'd ask you along, but talking makes her nervous.

JOHN:
 Yes, of course.

FRANKLIN:
 Good night, then.

JOHN:
 Good night.

 Franklin goes. It has grown dark. John stands for a moment, lost in thought. Then he turns and looks up at the lighted window, just as Jefferson's violin is heard playing a lush arpeggio. An instant later the light goes out.

 Incredible.

 Music begins.

 Oh, Abigail—

 Abigail appears, as before.

 I'm very lonely, Abigail.

ABIGAIL:
 Are you, John? Then as long as you were sending for wives, why didn't you send for your own?

JOHN:
 Don't be unreasonable, Abigail.

ABIGAIL:
 Now I'm unreasonable—you must add that to your list.

JOHN:
 List?

ABIGAIL:
 The catalogue of my faults you included in your last letter.

JOHN:
 They were fondly intended, madame!

SCENE 4 / **1776** 71

ABIGAIL:

That I play at cards badly?

JOHN:

A compliment!

ABIGAIL:

That my posture is crooked?

JOHN:

An endearment!

ABIGAIL:

That I read, write, and think too much?

JOHN:

An irony!

ABIGAIL:

That I am *pigeon-toed?*

JOHN:

Ah, well, there you have me, Abby—I'm afraid you *are* pigeon-toed. [*Smiling:*] Come to Philadelphia, Abigail—please come.

ABIGAIL:

Thank you, John, I do want to. But you know it's not possible now. The children have the measles.

JOHN:

Yes, so you wrote—Tom and little Abby.

ABIGAIL:

Only now it's Quincy and Charles. And it appears the farm here in Braintree is failing, John—the chickens and geese have all died and the apples never survived the late frost. How do you s'pose *she* managed to get away?

JOHN, *with a glance to the shuttered window:*

The winters are softer in Virginia.

ABIGAIL:

And their women, John?

JOHN:

Fit for Virginians, madame, but pale, puny things
beside New England girls!

ABIGAIL, *pleased:*

John! I thank you for that.

A pause.

JOHN:

How goes it with you, Abigail?

ABIGAIL:

Not well, John—not at all well.

She sings:

I live like a nun in a cloister,
Solitary, celibate, I hate it.
(And you, John?)

JOHN, *singing:*
Hm!
I live like a monk in an abbey,
Ditto, ditto, I hate it.

ABIGAIL:

Write to me with sentimental effusion,
Let me revel in romantic illusion.

JOHN:

Do y'still smell of vanilla and spring air?
And is my fav'rite lover's pillo' still firm and fair?

ABIGAIL:

What was there, John!
Still in there, John!

Come soon as you can to my cloister.
I've forgotten the feel of your hand.

JOHN:

> Soon, Madame, we shall walk in Cupid's grove to-
> gether . . .

JOHN AND ABIGAIL:

> And we'll fondly survey that promised land!
> Till then, till then,
>
> I am, as I ever was, and ever shall be,
> Yours . . .
> Yours . . .
> Yours . . .
> Yours . . .
> Yours . . .

ABIGAIL, *beating him to it:*

> Saltpetre, John! [*And she goes.*]
>
> *John smiles, Now the daylight returns; it's the next
> morning. Franklin enters.*

FRANKLIN:

> Sorry to be late, John—I was up till all hours.
> Have y'been here long?

JOHN:

> Not long.

FRANKLIN:

> And what're y'doing out here? I expected you'd be
> up there cracking the whip.

JOHN:

> The shutters are still closed.

FRANKLIN:

> My word, so they are! Well, as the French say—

JOHN:

> Oh, *please,* Franklin! Spare me your bawdy mind
> first thing in the morning!
>
> *They regard the closed shutters.*
>
> Dare we call?

FRANKLIN:
  A Congressman dares anything. Go ahead.

JOHN:
  Me?

FRANKLIN:
  Your voice is more piercing.

JOHN—*he starts, then hesitates:*
  This is positively indecent!

FRANKLIN:
  Oh, John, they're young and they're in love.

JOHN:
  Not them, Franklin—us! Standing out here—[*he gestures vaguely at the shuttered room*]—waiting for them to—I mean, what will people think?

FRANKLIN:
  Don't worry, John. The history books will clean it up.

JOHN:
  It doesn't matter. I won't appear in the history books, anyway—only you. [*He thinks about it.*] Franklin did this, Franklin did that, Franklin did some other damned thing. Franklin smote the ground, and out sprang George Washington, fully grown and on his horse. Franklin then electrified him with his miraculous lightning rod, and the three of them—Franklin, Washington, *and* the horse—conducted the entire Revolution all by themselves.
  A pause.

FRANKLIN:
  I like it!

  Now the shutter opens and Martha appears, dressed and radiant. She is humming a tune.

  Look at her, John—just look at her!

JOHN, *hypnotized:*

    I am.

FRANKLIN:

    She's even more magnificent than I remember! Of
    course, we didn't see much of her front last night.
    [*Calling:*] Good morrow, madame!

    She looks down at him blankly.

JOHN:

    Good morrow!

MARTHA:

    Is it the habit in Philadelphia for strangers to shout
    at ladies from the street?

FRANKLIN:

    Not at all, madame, but we're not—

MARTHA:

    And from men of your age it is not only unseemly,
    it's unsightly.

JOHN:

    Excuse me, madame, but we met last evening.

MARTHA:

    I spoke to no one last evening.

FRANKLIN:

    Indeed you did not, madame, but nevertheless we
    presented ourselves. This is Mr. John Adams and
    I am Dr. Franklin. [*As she stares at them, dum-
    founded:*] Inventor of the stove?

MARTHA:

    Oh, please, I know your names very well. But you
    say you presented yourselves?

FRANKLIN, *smiling:*

    It's of no matter. Your thoughts were well taken
    elsewhere.

MARTHA, *turning to the room for a moment:*
> My husband is not yet up.

FRANKLIN:
> Shall we start over? Please join us, madame.

MARTHA:
> Yes, of course. [*She disappears from the window.*]

FRANKLIN:
> No wonder the man couldn't write. Who could think of independence, married to her?

She appears, smiling.

MARTHA:
> I beg you to forgive me. It is indeed an honor meeting the two greatest men in America.

FRANKLIN, *smiling back:*
> Certainly the greatest within earshot, anyway.

MARTHA:
> I am not an idle flatterer, Dr. Franklin. My husband admires you both greatly.

FRANKLIN:
> Then we are doubly flattered, for we admire very much that which your husband admires.

A pause as they regard each other warmly. They have hit it off.

JOHN—*finally; the bull in the china shop:*
> Did you sleep well, madame? [*Franklin nudges him with his elbow.*] I mean, did you lie comfortably? Oh, damn! Y'know what I mean!

FRANKLIN:
> Yes, John, we do. Tell us about yourself, madame; we've had precious little information. What's your first name?

MARTHA:
Martha.

FRANKLIN:
Ah. Martha. He might at least have told us that.
I'm afraid your husband doesn't say very much.

JOHN:
He's the most silent man in Congress. I've never
heard him utter three sentences together.

FRANKLIN:
Not everyone's a talker, John.

MARTHA:
It's true, you know. [*She turns to look at the window.*] Tom is not—a talker.

She sings.

Oh, he never speaks his passions,
He never speaks his views.
Whereas other men speak volumes,
The man I love is mute.

In truth
I can't recall
Being woo'd with words
At all.

Even now . . .

Music continues under.

JOHN, *speaking:*
Go on, madame.

FRANKLIN:
How did he win you, Martha, and how does he
hold onto a bounty such as you?

MARTHA:
Surely you've noticed that Tom is a man of many
accomplishments: author, lawyer, farmer, archi-

tect, statesman—[*she hesitates*]—and still one more
that I hesitate to mention.

JOHN:
Don't hesitate, madame—don't hesitate!

FRANKLIN:
Yes, what *else* can that redheaded tombstone do?

MARTHA—*she looks at them for a moment, then leans
in and sings, confidentially:*
He plays the violin
He tucks it right under his chin,
And he bows,
Oh, he bows,
For he knows,
Yes, he knows, that it's . . .

Heigh, heigh, heigh diddle-diddle,
'Twixt my heart, Tom, and his fiddle,
My strings are unstrung.
Heigh-heigh-heigh-heigh-igh-igh . . .
Heigh—I am undone!

*John and Franklin look at one another, not at all
sure if she's putting them on or not.*

FRANKLIN, *speaking:*
The *violin,* madame?

MARTHA:
I hear his violin,
And I get that feeling within,
And I sigh . . .
Oh, I sigh . . .
He draws near,
Very near, and it's . . .

Heigh, heigh, heigh diddle-diddle, and . . .
Good-bye to the fiddle!
My strings are unstrung.

Heigh-heigh-heigh-heigh-igh-igh . . .
Heigh—I'm always undone!

FRANKLIN, *speaking:*
That settles it, John, we're taking up the violin!

JOHN, *to Martha:*
Very well, madame, you've got us playing the violin!
What happens next?

MARTHA:
Next, Mr. Adams?

JOHN:
Yes! What does Tom do now?

MARTHA, *demurely:*
Why, just what you'd expect.

John and Franklin exchange expectant looks.

We dance!

JOHN AND FRANKLIN, *together and to each other:*
Dance?

FRANKLIN:
Incredible!

MARTHA:
One-two-three, one-two-three!

*And in an instant she has swept Franklin off into
an energetic waltz. John watches them for a moment, still trying to understand.*

JOHN:
Who's playing the violin?

FRANKLIN:
Oh, John—really!

And Martha leaves Franklin to begin waltzing with

John, who, to Franklin's astonishment, turns out to dance expertly.

John! You can dance!

JOHN, *executing an intricate step—he is having a grand time:*

We still do a few things in Boston, Franklin!

Finally they have twirled and spun and danced themselves out.

MARTHA, *singing, as she catches her breath:*
When Heaven calls to me,
Sing me no sad elegy!
Say I died
Loving bride,
Loving wife,
Loving life. Oh, it was . . .

MARTHA, JOHN, AND FRANKLIN:
Heigh, heigh, heigh diddle-diddle . . .

MARTHA:
'Twixt my heart, Tom, and his
Fiddle, and
Ever 'twill be
Heigh-heigh-heigh-heigh-igh-igh . . .
Heigh, through eternity.

FRANKLIN, *in counterpoint:*
He plays the violin . . .

JOHN, *in counterpoint:*
He plays the violin . . .

MARTHA, *in counterpoint:*
He plays the violin!

They bow to her, and she curtsies.
Now Jefferson appears, a fiddle under his arm, and stuck on the end of his bow is a paper. He col-

*lects his wife, and together they start back toward
the room.*

JOHN:

Franklin, look! He's written something—he's done
it! [*He dashes after them, snatches the paper off the
bow, and comes back to Franklin, delighted, and
reads it.*] "Dear Mr. Adams: I am taking my wife
back to bed. Kindly go away. Y'r ob'd't, T. Jefferson."

FRANKLIN:

What, again?

JOHN:

Incredible!

FRANKLIN:

Perhaps I'm the one who should've written the
declaration, after all. At my age there's little doubt
that the pen is mightier than the sword.

He sings:

For it's
Heigh, heigh, heigh diddle-diddle.

Enviously:

And God bless the man who can fiddle . . .

JOHN, *ever the old warhorse:*
An independency!

JOHN AND FRANKLIN, *regaining their energy:*
Heigh-heigh-heigh-heig-igh-igh.
Yata-ta-ta-tah!
Through eternity!

And they exit arm in arm.

He plays the violin . . . Violin! . . . Violin! . . .

SCENE 5

The Chamber, as before

At rise, Congress is in session, though in an exceedingly loose manner. While Secretary Thomson delivers a droning report, it is clear that no one is listening. Hancock sits at the President's table, but he is occupied reading the Philadelphia Gazette, *his feet up on the desk; one group of Congressmen— Morris, Read, Wilson, and Dickinson—sit with their heads together, talking; another group—Hopkins, Bartlett, and Sherman—stands in the rear, also conversing; Rutledge and Hewes pace back and forth across the length of the Chamber as they talk; McKean stands by the window, cleaning a long rifle; Chase, a large napkin tied around his neck, sits eating a complete meal; Witherspoon is asleep at his desk, his head thrown back, his mouth open and snoring; and McNair is kept hopping from one group to another on this errand and that. The wall calendar now reads: "JUNE 22."*

THOMSON:

. . . and what follows is a complete and up-to-date list of the committees of this Congress now sitting, about to sit, or just having sat: A committee formed to investigate a complaint made against the quality of yeast manufactured at Mr. Henry Pendleton's mill, designated as the Yeast Committee; a committee formed to consider the most effective method of dealing with spies, designated as the Spies Committee; a committee formed to think, perhaps to do, but in any case to gather, to meet, to confer, to talk, and perhaps even to re-

solve that each rifle regiment be allowed at least
one drum and one fife attached to each company,
designated as the Drum and Fife Committee; a
committee formed to . . .

*Franklin and Dr. Hall have entered and now stand
surveying the room.*

FRANKLIN:
Look at it, doctor—democracy! What Plato called
a "charming form of government, full of variety
and disorder." I never knew Plato had been to
Philadelphia.

HANCOCK, *as he reads the newspaper:* ·
McNair! Open that damn window!

HOPKINS, *joining Franklin and Hall, a mug of rum in
his hand:*
Ben, I want y'to see some cards I've gone 'n' had
printed up that ought t'save everybody here a whole
lot of time 'n' effort, considering the epidemic of
bad disposition that's been going around lately.
[*He reads:*] "Dear sir: You are without any doubt
a rogue, a rascal, a villain, a thief, a scoundrel, and
a mean, dirty, stinking, sniveling, sneaking, pimp-
ing, pocket-picking, thrice double-damned, no good
son-of-a-bitch"—and y'sign y'r name. What do
y'think?

FRANKLIN, *delighted:*
Stephen, I'll take a dozen right now!

THOMSON:
 . . . a committee formed to answer all Congressional correspondence designated as the Congressional correspondence Committee . . .

John strides in and joins Franklin.

JOHN:

> All right, Franklin, enough socializing—there's work to be done!

FRANKLIN, *pointedly:*

> Good morning, John!

JOHN:

> What? Oh. [*Waving it aside:*] Good morning, good morning. Now, then, let's get to it.

FRANKLIN:

> Let's get to what?

JOHN, *indicating the tally board:*

> Unanimity, of course. Look at that board—six nays to win over in little more than a week!

THOMSON:

> . . . a committee formed to consider the problem of counterfeit money, designated as the Counterfeit Money Committee . . .

FRANKLIN:

> All right, John, where do we start?

JOHN:

> How about Delaware? It's a sad thing to find her on the wrong side after all this time. Is there any news of Rodney?

FRANKLIN, *pointing:*

> McKean's back.

JOHN:

> Thomas!

> *They go to him.*

THOMSON:

> . . . a committee formed to study the causes of our military defeat in Canada, designated as the Military Defeat Committee . . .

JOHN:

How did you leave Caesar? Is he still alive?

McKEAN:

Aye, but the journey to Dover was fearful hard on
him. He never complained, but I could see the poor
man was sufferin'.

FRANKLIN:

But you got him safely home.

McKEAN:

I did, but I doubt he'll ever set foot out of it again.

JOHN:

That leaves you and Read split down the middle.
Will he come over?

McKEAN:

I don't know. He's a stubborn little snot!

JOHN:

Then work on him. Keep at him till you wear him
down!

McKEAN:

Och, John, face facts, will y'? If it were just Read
standin' in our way it wouldn't be so bad. But
look for yourself, man—[indicating the tally
board]—Mary-land, Pennsylvania, the entire
South—it's impossible!

JOHN:

It's imposible if we all stand around complaining
about it. To work, McKean—one foot in front of
the other.

FRANKLIN:

I believe I put it a better way: "Never leave off
till tomorrow that which you can do—"

JOHN:

Shut up, Franklin!

McKEAN:

But what good will it do? Y'know Dickinson—
he'll never give in! And y'haven't heard the last
of Rutledge yet, either.

JOHN:

Never mind about them. Your job is George Read.
Talk him deaf if you have to, but bring us back
Delaware!

McKEAN:

There's a simpler way. [*He holds up his rifle.*]
This'll break the tie! [*He goes to talk to Read.*]

FRANKLIN:

All right, John, who's next?

Again they turn to study the board.

THOMSON:

. . . a committee formed to keep secrets, designated as the Secrets Committee . . .

JOHN:

Pennsylvania and Mary-land. I suggest you try to
put your own house in order while I take a crack
at Old Bacon Face (look at him stuff himself!)
Mr. Chase! [*He goes to him.*] How about it, Chase?
When are you coming to your senses?

CHASE, *sourly:*

Please, Mr. Adams—not while I'm eating!

FRANKLIN, *drawing Wilson aside:*

Mr. Wilson, it's time to assert yourself. When you
were a judge, how in hell did you ever make a
decision?

WILSON:

The decisions I made were all based on legality
and precedence. But there is no legality here—
and certainly no precedent.

FRANKLIN:

Because it's a new idea, you clot! We'll be setting our own precedent!

READ, *arguing with McKean:*

No, Mr. McKean—no, no, *no!*

McKEAN:

Damn y'r eyes, Read, y'came into this world screamin' "no," and y're determined to leave it the same way, y'little worm!

JOHN, *with Chase:*

The Congress is waiting on you, Chase—America's waiting—the whole *world* is waiting! What's that, kidney? [*He takes a morsel of food from Chase's plate with his fingers, but Chase slaps his hand and he drops it.*]

CHASE:

Leave me alone, Mr. Adams, you're wasting your time. If I thought we could win this war, I'd be at the front of your ranks. But you must know it's impossible! You've heard General Washington's dispatches. His army has fallen apart.

JOHN:

Washington's exaggerating the situation in order to arouse this torpid Congress into action. Why, as Chairman of the War Committee I can tell you for a fact that the army has never been in better shape! Never have troops been so cheerful! Never have soldiers been more resolute! Never have discipline and training been more spirited!

The Courier enters, dusty as ever. John winces.

Good God!

The Courier deposits his dispatch on Thomson's

desk and goes. Hancock puts down his paper and
pounds the gavel.

HANCOCK:
May we have your ears, gentlemen? Mr. Thomson has a dispatch.

Everyone turns to listen. Witherspoon is nudged
awake.

THOMSON, *ringing his bell:*
From the Commander, Army of the United Colonies; in New York, dispatch number one thousand,
one hundred and fifty-seven. "To the honorable
Congress, John Hancock, President. Dear Sir:
It is with the utmost despair that I must report
to you the confusion and disorder that reign in
every department—"

McNAIR:
Sweet Jesus!

THOMSON:
"The Continental soldier is as nothing ever seen
in this, or any other, century; he is a misfit, igno-
rant of hygiene, destructive, disorderly and totally
disrespectful of rank. Only this last is understand-
able as there is an incredible reek of stupidity
amongst the officers. The situation is most desperate at the New Jersey Training Ground in New
Brunswick where every able-bodied whore—*whore*
—in the Colonies has assembled. There are constant reports of drunkenness, desertion, foul lan-
guage, naked bathing in the Raritan River, and an
epidemic of the French disease. I have declared the
town 'off-limits' to all military personnel—with
the exception of officers. I beseech the Congress
to dispatch the War Committee to this place in

the hope of restoring some of the order and discipline we need to survive. Y'r ob'd't—

Drum roll.

—G. Washington."

MCKEAN:

Och! The man would depress a hyena!

HANCOCK:

Well, Mr. Adams, you're Chairman of the War
Committee. Do y'feel up to whoring, drinking,
deserting, and New Brunswick?

WITHERSPOON:

There must be some mistake. I have an aunt who
lives in New Brunswick!

Laughter.

DICKINSON:

You must tell her to keep up the good work!

Laughter.

Come, come, Mr. Adams, you must see that it's
hopeless. Let us recall General Washington and
disband the Continental Army before we are over-
whelmed.

JOHN:

Oh, yes, the English would like that, wouldn't
they?

DICKINSON:

Why not ask them yourself? They ought to be here
any minute.

Laughter.

RUTLEDGE:

And when they hang you, Mr. Adams, I hope you
will put in a good word for the rest of us.

A distressed silence.

CHASE:

> Face facts, Mr. Adams—a handful of drunk and
> disorderly recruits against the entire British Army,
> the finest musketmen on earth. How can we win?
> How can we even hope to survive?

JOHN:

> Answer me straight, Chase. If you thought we
> *could* beat the redcoats, would Mary-land say
> "yea" to independence?

CHASE:

> Well, I suppose—

JOHN:

> No supposing, Chase—would you or wouldn't
> you?

CHASE:

> Very well, Mr. Adams—yes, we would.

JOHN:

> Then come with me to New Brunswick and see for
> yourself!

MCKEAN:

> John! Are y'mad?

BARTLETT:

> Y'heard what Washington said—it's a shambles!

HOPKINS:

> They're pushin' y'into it, Johnny!

JOHN:

> What do y'say, Chase?

MORRIS:

> Go ahead, Sam. It sounds lively as hell up there.

CHASE:

> All right—why not? And maybe it'll be John
> Adams who comes to his senses.

JOHN:

Mr. President, the War Committee will heed General Washington's request! A party consisting of Mr. Chase, Dr. Franklin, and myself will leave immediately.

HANCOCK:

Is that satisfactory with you, Dr. Franklin?

All eyes turn to Franklin, who is asleep again. Hopkins nudges him.

JOHN:

Wake up, Franklin, you're going to New Brunswick!

FRANKLIN:

Like hell I am. What for?

HOPKIN:

The whoring and the drinking.

FRANKLIN, *perking up:*

Why didn't you say so?

They start out. John driving them ahead of him like a sergeant-major.

JOHN:

Come on, Chase, move all that lard! We've no time to lose! Left-right, left-right, left-right—!

And they are gone.

The other liberals then go, leaving only the conservatives. Dickinson looks around, then rises.

DICKINSON:

Mr. McNair, all this talk of independence has left a certain foulness in the air.

Laughter from the conservatives.

My friends and I would appreciate it if you could open some windows.

MCNAIR:
> What about the flies?

DICKINSON, *smiling:*
> The windows, Mr. McNair.

> *As McNair goes to the windows, the clock strikes four. Dickinson takes a deep breath, surveys the Chamber, then sings.*

> Oh, say, do you see what I see?
> Congress sitting here in sweet serenity.
> I could cheer.
> The reason's clear:
> For the first time in a year
> Adams isn't here!
> And, look!
> The sun is in the sky,
> The breeze is blowing by,
> And there's not a single fly!

> Oh, sing Hosanna, Hosanna!

CONSERVATIVES:
> Hosanna, Hosanna!

DICKINSON:
> And it's cool!

> Oh, ye cool, cool conservative men,
> Our like may never ever be seen again.
> We have land,
> Cash in hand,
> Self-command,
> Future planned.
> Fortune thrives,
> Society survives,
> In neatly ordered lives
> With well-endowered wives.

CONSERVATIVES:
>   Come sing Hosanna, Hosanna!

DICKINSON:
>   In our breeding and our manner ...

CONSERVATIVES:
>   ... We are cool!

>   *The cool, cool conservative men—Rutledge, Wil-*
>   *son, Read, Morris, Hall, Livingston, and Hewes*
>   *among them—elegantly prepare to dance.*

DICKINSON:
>   Come, ye cool, cool considerate set,
>   We'll dance together to the same minuet,
>   To the right,
>   Ever to the right,
>   Never to the left,
>   Forever to the right,
>   Let our creed,
>   Be never to exceed,
>   Regulated speed,
>   No matter what the need!

CONSERVATIVES:
>   Come sing Hosanna, Hosanna!

DICKINSON:
>   Emblazoned on our banner
>   Is "Keep Cool!"

>   *The Minuet is led by Dickinson and Rutledge, as*
>   *the conservatives dance. During this the Courier*
>   *re-enters and deposits his dispatch, as usual, on*
>   *Thomson's desk. McNair goes to him, offers him*
>   *a rum, and he stays.*

CONSERVATIVES:
>   To the right,
>   Ever to the right,

Never to the left,
Forever to the right.

DICKINSON:

Hands attach,
Tightly latch,
Everybody match.

THOMSON, *singing:*

I have a new dispatch . . .

Music stops, but the Minuet continues silently.
Thomson speaks.

From the Commander, Army of the United Colonies; in New York, dispatch number one thousand,
one hundred and fifty-eight. "To the honorable
Congress, John Hancock, President. Dear Sir: I
awoke this morning to find that Gen. Howe has
landed twenty-five thousand British regulars and
Hessian mercenaries on Staten Island and that the
fleet, under the command of his brother, Admiral
Lord Howe, controls not only the Hudson and
East Rivers, but New York Harbour, which now
looks like all of London afloat. I can no longer,
in good conscience, withhold from the Congress
my certainty that the British military object at this
time is Philadelphia. Happy should I be if I could
see the means of preventing them, but at present
I confess I do not. Oh, how I wish I had never
seen the Continental Army. I would have done
better to retire to the back country and live in a
wigwam. Y'r ob'd't—

Drum roll.

—G. Washington."

A short pause; then music begins again and the
song continues as if nothing had happened.

CONSERVATIVES, *singing:*
What we do, we do rationally.

DICKINSON:
We never ever go off half
cocked, not we.

CONSERVATIVES:
Why begin,
Till we know that we can win?
And if we cannot win,
Why bother to begin?

RUTLEDGE:
We say this game's not of our choosing,
Why should we risk losing?

CONSERVATIVE:
We cool, cool men.

DICKINSON, *speaking, still dancing:*
Mr. Hancock, you're a man of property—one of
us. Why don't you join us in our minuet? Why do
you persist in dancing with John Adams? Good
Lord, sir, you don't even like him!

HANCOCK, *singing:*
That is true,
He annoys me quite a lot,
But still I'd rather trot
To Mr. Adams' new gavotte.

DICKINSON, *speaking, continuing to dance:*
But why? For personal glory? For a place in history? Be careful, sir. History will brand him and
his followers as traitors!

HANCOCK:
Traitors to what, Mr. Dickinson—the British
Crown? Or the British *half*-crown? Fortunately,

there are not enough men of property in America
to dictate policy.

DICKINSON:

Perhaps not, but don't forget that most men with
nothing would rather protect the possibility of becoming rich than face the reality of being poor.
And that is why they will follow us . . .

CONSERVATIVES:

. . . To the right,
Ever to the right,
Never to the left,
Forever to the right.
Where there's gold,
A market that will hold,
Tradition that is old,
A reluctance to be bold.

DICKINSON:

I sing Hosanna, Hosanna!
In a sane and lucid manner!

CONSERVATIVES:

We are cool!

We're the cool, cool considerate men,
Whose like may never ever be seen again!
With our land,
Cash in hand,
Self-command,
Future planned.

And we'll hold
To our gold,
Tradition that is old,
Reluctant to be bold!

We say this game's not of our choosing.
Why should we risk losing?

We Cool, Cool, Cool, Cool, Cool,
    Cool, Cool, Cool, Cool, Cool,
    Cool—!
    Cool—!
    Men!!

They turn and go, leaving only McNair, the Leather Apron, and the Courier in the Chamber. They are silent for a moment.

MCNAIR:
How'd you like to try 'n' borrow a dollar from one o' them? [*To the Courier:*] Want another rum, Gen'rul?

COURIER:
Gen'rul? [*He grins.*] Lord, I ain't even a *corp'l.*

MCNAIR:
Yeah, well, what's the Army know? [*He pours the the Courier another drink, pours himself and the Leather Apron a pair, selects one of Hancock's good clay pipes, lights it, then bangs with the gavel.*] Sit down, gentlemen. The Chair rules it's too damn hot to work! [*He occupies one chair, the Courier another, and the Leather Apron still a third.*] What's it like out there, Gen'rul?

COURIER:
You prob'ly know more'n me.

MCNAIR:
Sittin' in here? Sweet Jesus! This is the *last* place to find out what's goin' on!

LEATHER APRON, *to the Courier:*
I'm aimin' t'join up!

MCNAIR:
What're you talkin' about? You don't have to join up—you're in the Congress!

LEATHER APRON:
   What's that got t'do with it?

MCNAIR:
   Y'don't see *them* rushin' off t'get killed, do you?
   But they sure are great ones f'r sendin' others, I'll
   tell you that.

COURIER, *indicating his chair:*
   Who sets here?

MCNAIR:
   Caesar Rodney of Delaware. Where *you* from,
   Gen'rul?

COURIER:
   Watertown.

MCNAIR:
   Where's that?

COURIER:
   Massachusetts.

MCNAIR:
   Well, then, you belong down there. [*He indicates
   John's chair.*] But be careful; there's somethin'
   about that chair that makes a man awful noisy.
   *The Courier goes to Adams' chair and touches it
   reverently before he sits.*

LEATHER APRON:
   You seed any fightin'?

COURIER, *proudly:*
   Sure did. I seed my two best friends git shot dead
   on the very same day! Right on the village green
   it was, too! [*The recollection takes hold.*] An'
   when they didn't come home f'r supper, their
   mommas went down the hill lookin' for 'em.
   [*Music in, softly.*] Miz Lowell, she foun' Tim'thy

right off, but Miz Pickett, she looked near half
the night f'r Will'm cuz he'd gone 'n' crawled off
the green 'fore he died.

He is silent for a moment; then he sings.

Momma, hey, Momma,
Come lookin' for me.
I'm here in the meadow
By the red maple tree.
Momma, hey, Momma,
Look sharp—here I be.
Hey, Hey—
Momma, look sharp!

Them so'jurs, they fired,
Oh, Ma, did we run.
But then we turned round
An' the battle begun.
Then I went under—
Oh, Ma, am I done?
Hey, Hey—
Momma, look sharp!

My eyes are wide open,
My face to the sky.
Is that you I'm hearin'
In the tall grass nearby?
Momma, come find me
Before I do die.
Hey, Hey—
Momma, look sharp!

COURIER, MCNAIR, AND LEATHER APRON:
    I'll close y'r eyes, my Billy,
    Them eyes that cannot see,
    An' I'll bury ya, my Billy,
    Beneath the maple tree.

COURIER, *as McNair and Leather Apron hum quietly:*
    An' never ag'in
    Will y'whisper t'me,
    "Hey, Hey—"
    Oh, Momma, look sharp!

    The lights fade.

SCENE 6

An anteroom off the main Congressional Chamber.
At rise, the stage remains dark from the previous scene as the sounds of Congress in session are heard: first, Thomson's bell for attention.

HANCOCK:
The Secretary will now read the report of the Declaration Committee. Mr. Thomson.

THOMSON:
"A Declaration by the Representatives of the United States of America in General Congress assembled."

Lights come up on the anteroom. It is deserted save for Jefferson, who stands by the door into the Chamber, holding it ajar so he can listen to Thomson read his Declaration.

"When in the Course of Human Events, it becomes necessary for one People to dissolve the Political Bands which have connected them with another, and to assume among the Powers of the Earth, the separate and equal Station to which the Laws of Nature and of Nature's God entitle them, a decent respect to the Opinions of Mankind requires that they should declare the causes which impel them to the Separation. We hold these Truths to be self-evident, that all Men are created equal, that they are endowed by their Creator with certain inalienable Rights—"

Jefferson, having heard a sound offstage, closes the door, silencing Thomson's voice. John and Franklin enter from the wings, wearing capes and hats.

JOHN:

Jefferson! We're back and we've got Mary-land—
that is, we *will,* soon as Chase gets through telling
the Mary-land Assembly what we saw in New
Brunswick!

FRANKLIN:

He's in Annapolis right now, describing a ragtag
collection of provincial militiamen who couldn't
train together, drill together, or march together—
but when a flock of ducks flew by and they saw
their first dinner in three full days, sweet Jesus!
Could they *shoot* together! It was a slaughter!

JEFFERSON, *not listening:*

They're reading the Declaration.

JOHN:

What? How far have they got?

JEFFERSON:

". . . to render the Military independent of and
superior to the Civil Power."

John opens the door to the Chamber.

THOMSON:

". . . independent of and superior to—"

*John closes the door. The three men pace for a
moment.*

JOHN:

Well, there's nothing to fear. It's a masterpiece!
I'm to be congratulated.

FRANKLIN:

You?

JOHN:

For making him write it.

FRANKLIN:
>Ah, yes——of course.

>*They are silent for a moment; then ...*

JOHN, *singing:*
>It's a masterpiece, I say.
>They will cheer ev'ry word,
>Ev'ry letter!

JEFFERSON:
>I wish I felt that way.

FRANKLIN:
>I believe I can put it better!

>Now then, attend,
>As friend to friend,
>Our Declaration Committee——
>For us I see
>Immortality ...

ALL:
>In Philadelphia city.

FRANKLIN:
>A farmer,
>A lawyer,
>And a sage!——
>A bit gouty in the leg.
>You know, it's quite bizarre
>To think that here we are,
>Playing midwives to
>An egg.

JOHN, *speaking:*
>Egg? What egg?

FRANKLIN:
>America——the birth of a new nation!

JEFFERSON:

If only we could be sure what kind of a bird it's
going to be.

FRANKLIN:

Tom's got a point. What sort of a bird should we
choose as the symbol of our new America?

JOHN:

The eagle.

JEFFERSON:

The dove.

FRANKLIN:

The turkey.

*John and Jefferson look at Franklin in surprise,
then at each other.*

JOHN:

The eagle.

JEFFERSON:

The dove.

JOHN:

The *eagle!*

JEFFERSON, *shrugging:*
The eagle.

A pause.

FRANKLIN:

The turkey.

JOHN:

The eagle is a majestic bird.

FRANKLIN:

The eagle is a scavenger, a thief, a coward, and
the symbol of more than ten centuries of European
mischief.

JOHN:

>And the turkey?

FRANKLIN:

>A truly noble bird, a native of America, a source
>of sustenance to our settlers, and an incredibly
>brave fellow [*kettle drums*] who would not flinch
>from attacking an entire regiment of Englishmen
>singlehandedly! Therefore the national bird of
>America is going to be [*drums out*]—

JOHN:

>The eagle.

FRANKLIN AND JEFFERSON, *shrugging:*

>The eagle.

>*A pause.*

JOHN, *singing:*

>We're waiting for the . . .

ALL:

>Chirp! chirp! chirp!
>Of an eaglet being born,
>Waiting for the
>Chirp! chirp! chirp!
>On this humid Monday morning in this
>—Congressional incubator!

FRANKLIN:

>God knows, the temp'rature's hot enough
>To hatch a stone,
>Let alone
>An egg!

JOHN:

>We're waiting for the . . .

ALL:

>Scratch! scratch! scratch!

Of that tiny little fellow,
Waiting for the egg to hatch,
On this humid Monday morning in this
—Congressional incubator!

JOHN:

God knows the temp'rature's hot enough
To hatch a stone!

JEFFERSON:

But will it hatch
An egg?

JOHN, *speaking:*

The Declaration will be a triumph, I tell you—a
triumph! If I was ever sure of anything I'm sure
of that—a triumph!

A pause.

And if it isn't, we've still got four days left to think
of something else.

He sings.

The eagle's going to
Crack the shell
Of the egg that England laid!

ALL:

Yessir! We can
Tell! tell! tell!
On this humid Monday morning in this
—Congressional incubator!

FRANKLIN:

And just as Tom, here, has written,
Though the shell may belong to Great Britain,
The eagle inside
Belongs to us!

ALL:

> And just as Tom, here, has written,
> We say "To hell with Great Britain!"
> The eagle inside
> Belongs to us!!!

They turn and go confidently into the Chamber.

SCENE 7

The Chamber. Congress is in session—Hancock, Bartlett, Hopkins, Sherman, Morris, Livingston, Witherspoon, Dickinson, Wilson, McKean, Read, Hewes, Rutledge, and Hall being present—and now John, Franklin, and Jefferson take their places, this action continuing from the previous scene, as Thomson completes his reading of the Declaration. The calendar on the wall now reads: "JUNE 28."

THOMSON:

"—and that as Free and Independent States, they have full Power to levy War, conclude Peace, contract Alliances, establish Commerce, and to do all other Acts and Things which Independent States may of right do. And for the support of this Declaration we mutually pledge to each other our Lives, our Fortunes, and our sacred Honor."

Finished, he looks up. Nobody moves, nobody speaks, nobody reacts; the silence is complete and prolonged.

HANCOCK, *finally:*

Very well. Thank you, Mr. Thomson. The Congress has heard the report of the Declaration Committee. Are there any who wish to offer amendments, deletions, or alterations to the Declaration?

Suddenly every hand but John's, Franklin's, Jefferson's, and Hopkins' shoots up.

CONGRESS:

Mr. President!
Hear me, Mr. President!

I've got one!
Over here!
[*Et cetera.*]

HANCOCK, *pounding the gavel for order:*
Gentlemen, *please!* McNair, you'd better open the window. Colonel McKean, I saw your hand first.

McKEAN:
Mr. Jefferson, it's a bonny paper y've written, but somewhere in it y've mentioned "Scottish and foreign mercenaries sent t'destroy us." *Scottish,* Tom?

JOHN:
It's in reference to a Highland regiment which stood against us at Boston.

McKEAN:
Och, it was more likely Germans wearin' kilts to disguise their bein' there. I ask y'to remove the word and avoid givin' offense to a good people.

THOMSON:
Mr. Jefferson?

Jefferson nods and Thomson scratches his quill pen through the word. The many hands go up again.

HANCOCK:
The Reverend Witherspoon?

WITHERSPOON:
Mr. Jefferson, nowhere do you mention the Supreme Being. Certainly this was an oversight, for how could we hope to achieve a victory without His help? Therefore I must humbly suggest the following addition to your final sentence: "With a firm reliance on the protection of Divine Providence."

Again Thomson looks at Jefferson, who in turn looks at John; the two patriots shrug, then Jeffer-

*son turns back to Thomson and nods; the phrase
is added. More hands.*

HANCOCK:

Mr. Read?

READ:

Among your charges against the King, Mr. Jefferson, you accuse him of depriving us of the benefits of trial by jury. This is untrue, sir. In Delaware
we have always had trial by jury.

JOHN:

In Massachusetts we have not.

READ:

Oh. Then I suggest that the words "in many cases"
be added.

THOMSON:

Mr. Jefferson?

And again Jefferson nods; the words are added.

McKEAN:

"In many cases!"—och, brilliant! I s'pose every
time y'see those three words y'r puny little chest'll
swell up w'i pride over y'r great historical contribution!

READ:

It's more memorable than your unprincipled white-
wash of that race of barbarians!

HANCOCK, *pounding the gavel:*

Mr. Read, Colonel McKean—that's enough!

*The hands are raised, this time Hopkins' among
them.*

Mr. Hopkins?

HOPKINS:

No objections, Johnny, I'm just trying to get a drink.

HANCOCK:

I should've known. McNair, get him a rum.

Again the hands go up.

McNair crosses to the wall calendar and removes a leaf, uncovering "June 29."

Mr. Bartlett?

BARTLETT:

Mr. Jefferson, I beg you to remember that we still have friends in England. I see no purpose in antagonizing them with such phrases as "unfeeling brethren" and "enemies in war." Our quarrel is with the British King, not the British people.

JOHN:

Be sensible, Bartlett. Remove those phrases, and the entire paragraph becomes meaningless. And it so happens it's among the most stirring and poetic of any passage in the entire document. [*He picks up the Declaration from Thomson's desk, preparing to read.*]

BARTLETT:

We're a Congress, Mr. Adams, not a literary society. I ask that the entire paragraph be stricken.

THOMSON:

Mr. Jefferson?

And again, after some thought this time, and with some sadness, Jefferson nods.

JOHN:

Good God, Jefferson! Don't you ever intend to speak up for your own work?

JEFFERSON:

I had hoped that the work would speak for itself.

Thomson scratches out the paragraph.

McNAIR:

Mr. Hancock.

HANCOCK:

What is it, Mr. McNair?

McNAIR:

I can't say I'm very fond of the United States of America as a name for a new country.

HANCOCK:

I don't care *what* you're fond of, Mr. McNair. You're not a member of this Congress! Mr. Sherman?

SHERMAN, *coffee in hand, as usual:*

Brother Jefferson, I noted at least two distinct and direct references to the British Parliament in your Declaration. Do you think it's wise to alienate that august body in light of our contention that they have never had any direct authority over us anyway?

JOHN:

This is a revolution, dammit! We're going to have to offend *some*body!

FRANKLIN:

John. [*He leads John downstage as the debate in the Chamber continues silently behind them.*] John, you'll have an attack of apoplexy if you're not careful.

JOHN:

Have you heard what they're doing to it? Have *you heard?*

FRANKLIN:

> Yes, John, I've heard, but—

JOHN:

> And so far it's only been our friends? Can you imagine what our enemies will do?

HANCOCK:

> The word "Parliament" will be removed wherever it occurs.

JOHN:

> They won't be satisfied until they remove one of the Fs from Jefferson's name.

FRANKLIN:

> Courage, John! It won't last much longer.

> *They start back toward their seats as the hands go up again.*

> *And again McNair goes to the calendar and removes another page; it now reads: "JUNE 30."*

HANCOCK:

> Mr. Dickinson?

DICKINSON:

> Mr. Jefferson, I have very little interest in your paper, as there is no doubt in my mind that we have all but heard the last of it. But I am curious about one thing: why do you refer to King George as a tyrant?

JEFFERSON:

> Because he is a tyrant.

DICKINSON:

> I remind you, Mr. Jefferson, that this "tyrant" is still your King.

JEFFERSON:

> When a king becomes a tyrant he thereby breaks the contract binding his subjects to him.

DICKINSON:

How so?

JEFFERSON:

By taking away their rights.

DICKINSON:

Rights that came from him in the first place.

JEFFERSON:

All except one—the right to be free comes from nature.

DICKINSON:

Mr. Wilson, do we in Pennsylvania consider King George a tyrant?

WILSON:

Mmm? Well—I don't know. [*As he meets Dickinson's stone stare:*] Oh. No—no, we don't. He's not a tyrant—in Pennsylvania.

DICKINSON:

There you are, Mr. Jefferson. Your Declaration does not speak for us all. I demand the word "tyrant" be removed!

Thomson begins scratching it out.

JEFFERSON:

Just a moment, Mr. Thomson, I do not consent. The King is a tyrant whether we say so or not. We might as well say so.

THOMSON:

But I already scratched it out.

JEFFERSON, *forcefully:*

Then scratch it back in!

A surprised silence.

HANCOCK, *finally:*

> Put it back, Mr. Thomson. The King will remain a tyrant.

> *Once more McNair goes to the calendar and changes the date—to* "JULY 1."

> Mr. Hewes?

HEWES:

> Mr. Jefferson, nowhere do you mention deep-sea fishin' rights. We in North Carolina—

> *Everyone throws up his hands in disgust and impatience.*

JOHN:

> Good God! *Fishing* rights! How long is this piddling to go on? We have been sitting here for three full days. We have endured, by my count, eighty-five separate changes and the removal of close to four hundred words. Would you whip it and beat it till you break its spirit? I tell you this document is a masterful expression of the American mind!

> *There is a silence.*

HANCOCK:

> If there are no more changes, then, I can assume that the report of the Declaration Committee has been—

RUTLEDGE, *deliberately:*

> Just a moment, Mr. President.

FRANKLIN, *to John:*

> Look out.

RUTLEDGE:

> I wonder if we could prevail upon Mr. Thomson to read again a small portion of Mr. Jefferson's

Declaration—the one beginnin' "He has waged cruel war—"?

HANCOCK:

Mr. Thomson?

THOMSON, *reading back rapidly to himself:*

" . . . He has affected . . . He has combined . . . He has abdicated . . . He has plundered . . . He has constrained . . . He has excited . . . He has *in*cited . . . He has waged cruel war!" Ah. [*He looks up.*] Here it is. [*He clears his throat and reads.*] "He has waged cruel war against human nature itself, in the persons of a distant people who never offended him, captivating and carrying them into slavery in another hemisphere. Determined to keep open a market where men should be bought and sold, he has prostituted—"

RUTLEDGE:

That will suffice, Mr. Thomson, I thank you. Mr. Jefferson, I can't quite make out what it is you're talkin' about.

JEFFERSON:

Slavery, Mr. Rutledge.

RUTLEDGE:

Ah, yes. You're referrin' to us as slaves of the King.

JEFFERSON:

No, sir, I'm referring to *our* slaves. Black slaves.

RUTLEDGE:

Ah! Black slaves. Why didn't you say so, sir? Were you tryin' to hide your meanin'?

JEFFERSON:

No, sir.

RUTLEDGE:

Just another literary license, then.

JEFFERSON:

If you like.

RUTLEDGE:

I don't like at all, Mr. Jefferson. To us in South
Carolina, black slavery is our peculiar institution
and a cherished way of life.

JEFFERSON:

Nevertheless, we must abolish it. Nothing is more
certainly written in the Book of Fate than that this
people shall be free.

RUTLEDGE:

I am not concerned with the Book of Fate right
now, sir. I am more concerned with what's written
in your little paper there.

JOHN:

That "little paper there" deals with freedom for
Americans!

RUTLEDGE:

Oh, really! Mr. Adams is now callin' our black
slaves Americans. Are-they-now?

JOHN:

They are! They're people and they're here—if
there is any requirement, I've never heard of it.

RUTLEDGE:

They are here, yes, but they are not people, sir,
they are *property*.

JEFFERSON:

No, sir! They are people who are being treated as
property. I tell you the rights of human nature are
deeply wounded by this infamous practice!

RUTLEDGE, *shouting:*

Then see to your own wounds, Mr. Jefferson, for you are a—*practitioner*, are you not?

A pause. Rutledge has found the mark.

JEFFERSON:

I have already resolved to release my slaves.

RUTLEDGE:

Then I'm sorry, for you have also resolved the ruination of your personal economy.

JOHN:

Economy. Always economy. There's more to this than a filthy purse-string, Rutledge. It's an offense against man and God.

HOPKINS:

It's a stinking business, Mr. Rutledge—a stinking business!

RUTLEDGE:

Is it really, Mr. Hopkins? Then what's that I smell floatin' down from the North—could it be the aroma of *hy*-pocrisy? For who holds the other end of that filthy purse-string, Mr. Adams? [*To everyone:*] Our northern brethren are feelin' a bit tender toward our slaves. They don't keep slaves, no-o, but they're willin' to be considerable carriers of slaves—to others! They are willin', for the shillin' —[*rubbing his thumb and forefinger together*]— or haven't y'heard, Mr. Adams? Clink! Clink!

He sings.

Molasses to
Rum to
Slaves!
Oh, what a beautiful waltz!

You dance with us,
We dance with you, in
Molasses and
Rum and
Slaves!
[*Afro-rhythm.*]

Who sail the ships out of Boston,
Laden with Bibles and Rum?
Who drinks a toast
To the Ivory Coast,
"Hail, Africa! The slavers have come."
New England, with Bibles and Rum!

Then,
It's off with the Rum and the Bibles
Take on the Slaves, clink! clink!
Then,
Hail and farewell!
To the smell of the African
Coast!

Molasses to
Rum to
Slaves!
'Tisn't morals, 'tis money that saves!
Shall we dance to the sound
Of the profitable pound, in
Molasses and
Rum and
Slaves!

Who sail the ships out of Guinea,
Laden with Bibles and Slaves?
'Tis Boston can boast
To the West Indies coast:
"Jamaica! We brung what y'craves!
Antigua! Barbados!

We brung Bibles
And Slaves!"

He speaks, Afro-rhythm continues.

Gentlemen! You mustn't think our northern
friends merely see our slaves as figures on a ledger.
Oh, no, sir! They see them as figures on the block!
Notice the faces at the auctions, gentlemen—white
faces on the African wharves—New England faces,
seafaring faces: "Put them in the ships, cram them
in the ships, *stuff* them in the ships!" Hurry, gentlemen, let the auction begin!

He sings.

> Ya-ha . . .
> Ya-ha . . . ha-ma-ha-cundahhh!

Gentlemen, do y' hear?
That's the cry of the auctioneer!

> Ya-ha . . .
> Ya-ha . . . ha-ma-ha-cundahhh!

Slaves, gentlemen! Black gold, livin' gold—gold!
From:
Annn-go-laah!
Guinea-Guinea-Guinea!
Blackbirds for sale!

Aaa-shan-tiiii!
Ibo! Ibo! Ibo! Ibo!

Blackbirds for sale!
Handle them!
Fondle them!
But don't finger them!
They're prime, they're prime!

> Ya-ha . . .
> Ya-ha . . . ha-ma-ha-cundahhh!

Music stops.

BARTLETT, *pleading:*
>For the love of God, Mr. Rutledge, *please!*

>*Music resumes.*

RUTLEDGE:
>Molasses to
>Rum to
>Slaves!

>Who sail the ships back to Boston,
>Laden with gold, see it gleam?
>Whose fortunes are made
>In the triangle trade?
>Hail, Slavery, the New England
>Dream!

>Mr. Adams, I give you a toast!
>Hail, Boston!
>Hail, Charleston!
>Who *stinketh* the most?!

>*He turns and walks straight out of the Chamber.
>Hewes of North Carolina follows, and Hall of
>Georgia is right behind them.*

JOHN, *desperate:*
>Mr. Rutledge! Mr. Hewes! Dr. Hall!

>*Hall, the last, hesitates at the door as his name is
>called. He turns, looks at John, starts to say some-
>thing, then turns and goes after the others.*

WITHERSPOON:
>Don't worry, they'll be back.

McKEAN:
>Aye—t'vote us down.

>*There is a silence. Then Chase bursts into the
>Chamber.*

CHASE, *elated:*

It's done! Adams, Franklin—I have it! And the Mary-land Assembly's approved it! I told them about one of the greatest military engagements in history, against a flock of—

He runs down as the news is greeted with less enthusiasm than expected, and he sees the glum faces.

What's wrong? I thought—

DICKINSON, *cordially:*

You'll have to forgive them, Mr. Chase, they've just suffered a slight setback. And after all, what is a man profited, if he shall gain Mary-land, and lose the entire South? [*Smiling as he goes:*] Matthew, chapter sixteen, verse twenty-six.

Wilson, Read, Livingston, and Morris follow him out. Chase joins the ranks of the depressed as Thomson moves Maryland into the "Yea" column.

HANCOCK, *lifelessly:*

Mr. McNair—

McNAIR:

I know, the flies.

HANCOCK:

No—a rum.

JOHN, *surveying the sorry sight:*

Well? What're you all sitting around for? We're wasting time—precious time! [*To McKean:*] Thomas! I want you to ride down into Delaware and fetch back Caesar Rodney!

McKEAN:

John! Are y'mad? It's eighty miles on horseback, an' he's a dyin' man!

JOHN:

No! He's a patriot!

McKEAN:

Och, John, what good'll it do? The South's done
us in.

JOHN:

And suppose they change their minds—can we
get Delaware without Rodney?

McKEAN, *shaking his head:*

God! What a bastardly bunch we are! [*He goes.*]

JOHN, *turning to Hopkins:*

Stephen—

HOPKINS:

I'm goin' to the tavern, Johnny. If there's anything I can do for y'there, let me know. [*He goes.*]

JOHN:

Chase, Bartlett—

BARTLETT:

What's the use, John? The vote's tomorrow morning.

CHASE:

There's less than a full day left!

They go.

JOHN:

Roger!

SHERMAN:

Face facts, John—it's finished!

WITHERSPOON:

I'm sorry, John.

And they go.

John looks around, stunned by the defection.

*Only Franklin, Jefferson, Hancock, and Thomson
remain.*

FRANKLIN:

We've no other choice, John. The slavery clause
has to go.

JOHN:

Franklin, what are y'saying?

FRANKLIN:

It's a luxury we can't afford.

JOHN:

A luxury? A half-million souls in chains and Dr.
Franklin calls it a luxury! Maybe you should've
walked out with the South!

FRANKLIN:

You forget yourself, sir! I founded the first anti-
slavery society on this continent!

JOHN:

Don't wave your credentials at me! Perhaps it's
time you had them renewed!

FRANKLIN, *angrily:*

The issue here is independence! Maybe you've
lost sight of that fact, but I have not! How dare
you jeopardize our cause when we've come so far?
These men, no matter how much we disagree with
them, are not ribbon clerks to be ordered about;
they're proud, accomplished men, the cream of
their colonies—and whether you like it or not,
they and the people they represent will be a part
of the new country you'd hope to create! Either
start learning how to live with them or pack up
and go home—but in any case, stop acting like a
Boston fishwife!

*And he leaves John alone, returning upstage to
join Jefferson.*

John turns and comes downstage.

JOHN:

Good God, what's happened to me? John Adams,
the great John Adams, Wise Man of the East—
what have I come to? My law practice down the
the pipe, my farm mortgaged to the hilt—at a
stage in life when other men prosper I'm reduced
to living in Philadelphia.

Abigail appears, as before.

Oh, Abigail, what am I going to do?

ABIGAIL:

Do, John?

JOHN:

I need your help.

ABIGAIL:

You don't usually ask my advice.

JOHN:

Yes—well, there doesn't appear to be anyone else
right now.

ABIGAIL, *sighing:*

Very well, John, what is it?

JOHN:

The entire South has walked out of this Congress,
George Washington is on the verge of total annihilation, the precious cause for which I've labored
these several years has come to nothing, and it
seems—[*a pause*]—it seems I am obnoxious and
disliked.

ABIGAIL:

Nonsense, John.

JOHN:

That I am unwilling to face reality.

ABIGAIL:

Foolishness, John.

JOHN:

That I am pig-headed.

ABIGAIL, *smiling:*

Ah, well, there you have me, John. I'm afraid you *are* pig-headed.

He smiles; a pause.

JOHN:

Has it been any kind of a life for you, Abby? God knows I haven't given you much.

ABIGAIL:

I never asked for more. After all, I am Mrs. John Adams—that's quite a lot for one lifetime.

JOHN, *bitterly:*

Is it, Abby?

ABIGAIL:

Think of it, John! To be married to the man who is always first in line to be hanged!

JOHN:

Yes. The ag-i-ta-tor. [*Turning to her:*] Why, Abby? You must tell me what it is! I've always been dissatisfied, I know that; but lately I find that I *reek* of discontentment! It fills my throat and floods my brain, and sometimes—sometimes I fear that there is no longer a dream, but only the discontentment.

ABIGAIL:

Oh, John, can you really know so little about yourself? And can you think so little of me that you'd believe I married the man you've described?

Have you forgotten what you used to say to me?
I haven't. "Commitment, Abby—commitment!
There are only two creatures of value on the face
of this earth: those with a commitment, and those
who require the commitment of others." [*A pause.*]
Do you remember, John?

JOHN, *nodding:*
I remember.

*McNair enters, carrying two gaily beribboned kegs,
and thumps them down in front of John.*

MCNAIR:
Mr. Adams—

JOHN:
What?

MCNAIR:
These're for you.

JOHN:
Just a minute—what are they? What's in them?
Who sent them?

Music in, glissando.

ABIGAIL, *singing:*
Compliments of the Concord Ladies' Coffee Club,
And the Sisterhood of the Truro Synagogue,
And the Friday Evening Baptist Sewing Circle,
And the Holy Christian Sisters of Saint Clare—
All for you, John!
I am, as I ever was, and ever shall be . . .
Yours . . .
Yours . . .
Yours . . .
Yours—

JOHN, *speaking:*
Just a moment, Abigail—what's in those kegs?

ABIGAIL, *singing triumphantly:*
   Saltpetre, John! [*She blows a kiss and goes.*]

   John turns back to the Chamber.

JOHN:
   McNair! Go out and buy every damned pin in
   Philadelphia!

MCNAIR:
   Pin? What sort of pin?

JOHN:
   I don't know—whatever ladies use with their sewing! And take these kegs to the armory—hurry,
   man! [*Turning as McNair goes:*] Franklin, Jefferson, what are you just sitting around for?

FRANKLIN:
   John, didn't you hear a word that I said before?

JOHN:
   Never mind that. Here's what you've got to do—

FRANKLIN:
   John! I'm not even speaking to you!

JOHN:
   It's too late for that dammit! [*Music in, vigor-
   ously.*] There's work to be done!

   He sings.

   Time's running out!
   Get up!
   Get out of your chair!
   Tomorrow is here.
   Too late,
   Too late to despair!

   Jefferson! Talk to Rutledge, talk!
   If it takes all night,
   Keep talking.

JOHN AND JEFFERSON:
> Talk and talk and talk!

JOHN, *speaking:*
> You're both Southern aristocrats—gentlemen, If he'll listen to anybody, he'll listen to you!

> *He sings.*

> Franklin!
> Time's running out!

FRANKLIN:
> I know. Get out of my chair!
> Do I have to talk to Wilson?

JOHN:
> Yes, yes, you do!
> If it takes all night,
> Keep talking!

JOHN, FRANKLIN, AND JEFFERSON:
> Talk and talk and talk!

JOHN, *speaking:*
> Get him away from Dickinson, that's the only way to do it!

> *Franklin and Jefferson go. Music under.*

HANCOCK, *coming forward:*
> I'm still from Massachusetts, John; you know where I stand. I'll do whatever you say.

JOHN, *considering:*
> No, you're the President of Congress. You're a fair man, Hancock—stay that way.

> *The Courier enters and stops short as he comes face to face with John, who takes his dispatch and crosses up to Thomson's desk, where he hands it to the Secretary.*

Tell me, Mr. Thomson, out of curiosity, do you stand with Mr. Dickinson, or do you stand with me?

THOMSON, *holding up the dispatch:*

I stand with the General. Lately—I've had the oddest feeling that he's been—writing to *me*.

He reads, singing.

"I have been in expectation
Of receiving a reply
On the subject of my last fifteen dispatches.
Is anybody there?
Does anybody care?
Does anybody care?
Y'r humble & ob'd't—"

Drum roll; then it runs down as Thomson, unable to read the signature, rises and goes, thoroughly discouraged.

  It is growing dark outside. Hancock stands by the door, watching John, concerned.

HANCOCK:

Are y'hungry, John?

JOHN:

No, I think I'll stay.

HANCOCK:

G'night, then. [*He goes.*]

John looks around the Chamber, then goes to Thomson's desk and picks up the dispatch.

JOHN, *singing:*

"Is anybody there?
Does anybody care?"

He drops the dispatch.

Does anybody see what I see?

They want me to quit,
They say, "John, give up the fight!"
Still to England I say:
"Good night forever, good night!"

For I have crossed the Rubicon,
Let the bridge be burn'd behind me!
Come what may, come what may . . .
Commitment!

The croakers all say
We'll rue the day,
There'll be hell to pay in
Fiery Purgatory!

Through all the gloom,
Through all the gloom, I can
See the rays of ravishing light and
Glory!

Is anybody there?!
Does anybody care?!
Does anybody see
What I see?!

I see
Fireworks!
I see the Pageant and Pomp and Parade!
I hear the bells ringing out
I hear the cannons' roar!

I see Americans, *all* Americans,
Free! For evermore!

*He "comes to" and looks around, realizing that
it's dark and that he's alone.*

How quiet . . .
How quiet the Chamber is. . . .
How silent . . .
How silent the Chamber is. . . .

Is anybody there—?

He waits for an answer; there is none.

Does anybody care—?

Again, nothing.

Does anybody see—what I see?

Music out.

HALL, *speaking:*
Yes, Mr. Adams, I do.

John turns and discovers the Georgia delegate standing by the door, in the shadows.

JOHN:
Dr. Hall, I didn't know anyone was—

HALL:
I'm sorry if I startled you. I couldn't sleep. In trying to resolve my dilemma I remembered something I'd once read—"that a representative owes the People not only his industry, but his judgment, and he betrays them if he sacrifices it to their opinion." [*He smiles.*] It was written by Edmund Burke, a member of the British Parliament.

He walks to the tally board and moves the name of Georgia from the "Nay" to the "Yea" column. The two men regard each other for a moment.

It has been growing light outside and now the clock, offstage, chimes ten and the men of the Congress return silently, in single file, each with his own private thoughts, McKean supporting Rodney at the end.

Then Hancock pounds the gavel.

HANCOCK:
Very well. The Congress will now vote on Virginia's resolution on independence. [*To Rodney:*]

Thank you for coming, Caesar. And God bless you, sir.

Foot-stamping and other signs of approval from all.

Call the roll, Mr. Thomson. And I'd remind you, gentlemen, that a single "Nay" vote will defeat the motion. Mr. Thomson?

Thomson goes to the tally board. During the following, Franklin is deeply engaged in silent argument with Dickinson and Wilson, their heads remaining together.

THOMSON, *droning:*
New Hampshire—

BARTLETT:
New Hampshire says "Yea."

THOMSON:
New Hampshire says "Yea." Massachusetts—

JOHN:
Massachusetts says "Yea."

THOMSON:
Massachusetts says "Yea." Rhode Island—

HOPKINS:
Rhode Island says "Yea."

THOMSON:
Rhode Island says "Yea." Connecticut—

SHERMAN:
Connecticut says "Yea."

THOMSON:
Connecticut says "Yea." New York—

MORRIS:
New York abstains—courteously.

THOMSON:
New York abstains.

MORRIS, *disgusted and ashamed:*
Courteously.

THOMSON:
New Jersey—

WITHERSPOON:
New Jersey says "Yea."

THOMSON:
New Jersey says "Yea." Pennsylvania—[*As no one responds:*] Pennsylvania?

FRANKLIN:
Mr. Secretary, Pennsylvania isn't ready yet. Come back to us later. [*He returns to the argument.*]

THOMSON:
Pennsylvania passes. Delaware—

RODNEY, *as McKean helps him to his feet:*
Delaware, by majority vote—

McKEAN:
Aye!

RODNEY:
—says "Yea."

FRANKLIN:
Well done, sir.

THOMSON:
Delaware says "Yea."

And Delaware's marker on the tally board is moved into the "Yea" column.

Mary-land—

CHASE:
Mary-land says "Yea."

THOMSON:
Mary-land says "Yea." Virginia—

JEFFERSON:
Virginia says "Yea."

THOMSON:
Virginia says "Yea." North Carolina—

HEWES:
North Carolina yields to South Carolina!

THOMSON:
South Carolina—

RUTLEDGE, *rising, then turning to John:*
Well, Mr. Adams?

JOHN, *returning his stare:*
Well, Mr. Rutledge?

RUTLEDGE:
Mr. Adams, you must believe that I will do what
I have promised to do.

A pause.

JOHN:
What do y'want, Rutledge?

RUTLEDGE:
Remove the offendin' passage from your Declaration.

JOHN:
If we did that we'd be guilty of what we ourselves
are rebelling against.

RUTLEDGE:
Nevertheless, remove it or South Carolina will bury
now and forever your dream of independence.

FRANKLIN, *imploring:*
John, I *beg* you to consider what you're doing.

JOHN:

> Mark me, Franklin, if we give in on this issue, posterity will never forgive us.

FRANKLIN:

> That's probably true. But we won't hear a thing, John—we'll be long gone. And besides, what will posterity think we were—demigods? We're men— no more, no less—trying to get a nation started against greater odds than a more generous God would have allowed. John, first things first! Independence! America! For if we don't secure that, what difference will the rest make?

JOHN, *looking around, uncertain:*
> Jefferson, say something.

JEFFERSON:

> What else is there to do?

JOHN:

> Well, man, you're the one who wrote it!

JEFFERSON:

> I wrote *all* of it, Mr. Adams!

He goes to Thomson's table, takes up the quill pen, and scratches the passage from the Declaration. Then he returns to his seat.

> *John snatches up the Declaration, goes to Rutledge, and waves it under his nose.*

JOHN:

> There! There it is, Rutledge! You've got your slavery, and little good may it do you! Now vote, damn you!

RUTLEDGE, *unruffled:*
> Mr. Secretary, the fair colony of South Carolina says "Yea."

THOMSON:

South Carolina says "Yea."

HEWES, *jumping up:*

North Carolina says "Yea!"

THOMSON:

North Carolina says "Yea."

The two markers on the tally board are moved out of the "Nay" column. Only Pennsylvania remains there.

Georgia.

HALL:

Georgia says "Yea."

THOMSON:

Georgia says "Yea." Pennsylvania, second call—

DICKINSON:

Mr. President, Pennsylvania regrets all of the inconvenience that such distinguished men as Adams, Franklin, and Jefferson were put to just now. They might have kept their document intact, for all the difference it will make. Mr. President, Pennsylvania says—

FRANKLIN:

Just a moment! I ask that the delegation be polled.

DICKINSON:

Dr. Franklin, don't be absurd!

FRANKLIN:

A poll, Mr. President. It's a proper request.

HANCOCK:

Yes, it is. Poll the delegation, Mr. Thomson.

THOMSON:

Dr. Benjamin Franklin—

FRANKLIN:
   Yea!

THOMSON:
   Mr. John Dickinson—

DICKINSON:
   Nay!

THOMSON:
   Mr. James Wilson— [*As there is no response:*]
   Judge Wilson?

   All eyes turn to Wilson.

FRANKLIN:
   There it is, Mr. Wilson, it's up to you now—the
   whole question of American independence rests
   squarely on your shoulders. An entirely new nation, Mr. Wilson, waiting to be born or to die in
   birth, all on your say-so. Which will it be, Mr.
   Wilson? Every map-maker in the world is waiting
   for your decision!

DICKINSON:
   Come now, James, nothing has changed. We
   mustn't let Dr. Franklin create one of his confu-
   sions. The question is clear.

FRANKLIN:
   Most questions are clear when someone else has
   to decide them.

JOHN, *quietly, turning the screw:*
   It would be a pity for a man who handed down
   hundreds of wise decisions from the bench to be
   remembered only for the one unwise decision he
   made in Congress.

DICKINSON:
   James, you're keeping everybody waiting. The
   Secretary has called for your vote.

WILSON, *to Dickinson:*

Please don't push me, John, I know what you want
me to do. But Mr. Adams is correct about one
thing. *I'm* the one who'll be remembered for it.

DICKINSON:

What do you mean?

WILSON:

I'm different from you, John. I'm different from
most of the men here. I don't want to be remembered. I just don't want the responsibility!

DICKINSON:

Yes, well, whether you want it or not, James,
there's no way of avoiding it.

WILSON:

Not necessarily. If I go with them, I'll only be one
among dozens; no one will ever remember the
name of James Wilson. But if I vote with you, I'll
be the man who prevented American independence. I'm sorry, John—I just didn't bargain for
that.

DICKINSON:

And is that how new nations are formed—by a
nonentity trying to preserve the anonymity he so
richly deserves?

FRANKLIN:

Revolutions come into this world like bastard
children, Mr. Dickinson—half improvised and half
compromised. Our side has provided the compromise; now Judge Wilson is supplying the rest.

WILSON, *to Dickinson:*

I'm sorry, John. My vote is "Yea."

FRANKLIN:

Mr. Secretary, Pennsylvania says "Yea."

THOMSON:

Pennsylvania says "Yea."

*There is a stunned silence as all eyes go to the tally
board and Pennsylvania's marker is moved into the
"Yea" column.*

The count being twelve to none with one absten-
tion, the resolution on independence—[*surprised*]
—is adopted.

JOHN:

It's done. It's done.

A pause.

HANCOCK:

Mr. Thomson, is the Declaration ready to be
signed?

THOMSON:

It is.

HANCOCK:

Then I suggest we do so. And the Chair further
proposes for our mutual security and protection,
that no man be allowed to sit in this Congress without attaching his name to it.

All eyes now go to Dickinson.

DICKINSON:

I'm sorry, Mr. President, I cannot, in good conscience, sign such a document. I will never stop
hoping for our eventual reconciliation with England. But because, in my own way, I regard America no less than does Mr. Adams, I will join the
Army and fight in her defense—even though I believe that fight to be hopeless. Good-by, gentlemen.
[*He starts out.*]

JOHN:

> Gentlemen of the Congress, I say yea John Dickinson!

> *Dickinson stops as the members of Congress express their admiration for him by stamping their feet and banging their walking sticks on the floor. Then he goes and Hancock pounds the gavel.*

HANCOCK:

> Gentlemen, are there any objections to the Declaration being approved as it now stands?

JOHN:

> I have one, Mr. Hancock.

HANCOCK:

> *You,* Mr. Adams?

JOHN:

> Yes. Mr. Jefferson, it so happens the word is *un*-alienable, not *in*alienable.

JEFFERSON:

> I'm sorry, Mr. Adams, *in*alienable is correct.

JOHN, *his voice rising:*

> I happen to be a Harvard graduate—

JEFFERSON, *his voice also rising:*

> And *I* attended William and Mary—

HANCOCK, *pounding the gavel:*

> Gentlemen, please! Mr. Jefferson, will you yield to Mr. Adams' request?

> *A pause.*

JEFFERSON:

> No, sir, I will not.

JOHN:

> Oh, very well, I'll withdraw it.

FRANKLIN:

Good for you, John!

JOHN, *privately:*

I'll speak to the printer about it later.

HANCOCK:

Very well, gentlemen. [*He goes to Thomson's desk and picks up the quill.*] We are about to brave the storm in a skiff made of paper, and how it will end, God only knows. [*He signs with a flourish.*]

HOPKINS:

That's a pretty large signature, Johnny.

HANCOCK:

So Fat George in London can read it without his glasses!

Laughter.

All right, gentlemen, step right up, don't miss your chance to commit treason!

Laughter.

FRANKLIN:

Hancock's right. This paper is our passport to the gallows. But there's no backing out now. If we don't hang together, we shall most assuredly hang separately.

Laughter.

McKEAN, *patting his ample middle:*

In any case hanging won't be so bad—one snap and it'll be over—[*snap!*]—just like that! But look at Read, there—he'll be dancing a jig long after I'm gone!

Laughter.

HANCOCK:

> Gentlemen, forgive me if I don't join in the merriment, but if we're arrested now—my name is still the only one *on* the damn thing!

> *More laughter, which subsides slowly as the Courier enters, deposits his dispatch on Thomson's desk, and departs, turning to glance at John as he goes.*

THOMSON:

> From the Commander, Army of the United Colonies—[*he stops, looks up*]—Army of the United States—in New York, dispatch number one thousand, two hundred and nine. "To the Hon. Congress, John Hancock, President. Dear Sir: I can now report with some certainty that the eve of battle is near at hand. Toward this end I have ordered the evacuation of Manhattan and directed our defenses to take up stronger positions on the Brooklyn Heights. At the present time my forces consist entirely of Haslet's Delaware Militia and Smallwood's Mary-landers, a total of five thousand troops stand against—[*he hesitates in horrified astonishment*]—twenty-five thousand of the enemy —and I begin to notice that many of them are lads under fifteen and old men, none of whom could truly be called soldiers. One personal note to Mr. Lewis Morris of New York—I must regretfully report that his estates have been totally destroyed but that I have taken the liberty of transporting Mrs. Morris and eight of the children to Connecticut and safety. The four older boys are now enlisted in the Continental Army. As I write these words, the enemy is plainly in sight beyond the river. How it will end only Providence can direct

—but dear God! what brave men—I shall lose—
before this business ends. Y'r ob'd't—

Drum roll.

—G. Washington."

*There is a silence, during which McNair goes to the
calendar and removes the final leaf, revealing:
"*JULY 4."

*The light outside has dimmed; it is becoming
evening.*

HANCOCK, *finally:*
Very well, gentlemen. McNair, go ring the bell.

McNair goes.

MORRIS, *rising:*
Mr. President!

HANCOCK:
Mr. Morris?

MORRIS:
To hell with New York—I'll sign it anyway.

HANCOCK:
Thank you, Mr. Morris. Stephen, sit down.

HOPKINS, *who has been standing next to the Declaration
on Thomson's desk:*

No—I want t'remember each man's face as he
signs.

HANCOCK:
Very well. Mr. Thomson—

*As each name is called, the signer rises, comes to
the Secretary's desk, signs, then stands to one side.
The tolling Liberty Bell begins, offstage.*

THOMSON, *in measured tones:*
> New Hampshire, Dr. Josiah Bartlett.
> Massachusetts, Mr. John Adams.
> Rhode Island, Mr. Stephen Hopkins.
> Connecticut, Mr. Roger Sherman.
> New York, Mr. Lewis Morris.
> New Jersey, the Reverend John Witherspoon.
> Pennsylvania, Dr. Benjamin Franklin.
> Delaware, Mr. Caesar Rodney.

Hancock takes the Declaration to the infirm Rodney, then returns it to the table.

> Mary-land, Mr. Samuel Chase.
> Virginia, Mr. Thomas Jefferson.
> North Carolina, Mr. Joseph Hewes.
> South Carolina, Mr. Edward Rutledge.
> Georgia, Dr. Lyman Hall.

As the last man signs, the sound of the tolling Liberty Bell in the belfry above becomes almost deafening.

Then the scene freezes for a brief instant, and the pose of the familiar Pine-Savage engraving of this occasion has been captured.

A scrim curtain falls, the scene visible through it. Then as the back-light dims and the curtain is lit from the front, it becomes opaque and reveals the lower half of the Declaration, featuring the signatures.

CURTAIN

The Declaration of Independence
Historical Note by the Authors
Select Bibliography

THE DECLARATION
OF INDEPENDENCE *

A DECLARATION BY THE REPRESENTATIVES OF THE UNITED STATES OF AMERICA, IN *GENERAL* CONGRESS ASSEMBLED

When, in the course of human events, it becomes necessary for one people to dissolve the political bands which have connected them with another, and to assume among the powers of the earth the separate and equal station to which the laws of nature and of nature's God entitle them, a decent respect to the opinions of mankind requires that they should declare the causes which impel them to the separation.

We hold these truths to be self evident: that all men are created equal; that they are endowed by their Creator with CERTAIN [*inherent and*] inalienable rights; that among these are life, liberty, and the pursuit of happiness; that to secure these rights, governments are instituted among men, deriving their just powers from the consent of the governed; that whenever any form of government becomes destructive of these ends, it is the right of the people to alter or to abolish it, and to institute new government, laying its foundation on such principles, and organizing its powers in such form, as to them shall

* The parts of Jefferson's first draft that were later struck out by Congress are printed in italics and enclosed in brackets. Insertions are printed in capitals.

seem most likely to effect their safety and happiness.
Prudence, indeed, will dictate that governments long
established should not be changed for light and transient
causes; and accordingly all experience hath shown that
mankind are more disposed to suffer while evils are suf-
ferable, than to right themselves by abolishing the forms
to which they are accustomed. But when a long train of
abuses and usurpations, [*begun at a distinguished period
and*] pursuing invariably the same object, evinces a
design to reduce them under absolute despotism, it is
their right, it is their duty to throw off such government,
and to provide new guards for their future security.
Such has been the patient sufferance of these colonies;
and such is now the necessity which constrains them to
ALTER [*expunge*] their former systems of government.
The history of the present king of Great Britain is a
history of REPEATED [*unremitting*] injuries and usurpations, ALL HAVING [*among which appears no solitary fact to contradict the uniform tenor of the rest,
but all have*] in direct object the establishment of an absolute tyranny over these states. To prove this, let facts
be submitted to a candid world [*for the truth of which
we pledge a faith yet unsullied by falsehood*].

He has refused his assent to laws the most wholesome
and the necessary for the public good.

He has forbidden his governors to pass laws of im-
mediate and pressing importance, unless suspended in
their operation till his assent should be obtained; and,
when so suspended, he has utterly neglected to attend
to them.

He has refused to pass other laws for the accommo-
dation of large districts of people, unless those people
would relinquish the right of representation in the legislature, a right inestimable to them, and formidable to
tyrants only.

He has called together legislative bodies at places

unusual, uncomfortable, and distant from the depository of their public records, for the sole purpose of fatiguing them into compliance with his measures.

He has dissolved representative houses repeatedly [*and continually*] for opposing with manly firmness his invasions on the rights of the people.

He has refused for a long time after such dissolutions to cause others to be elected, whereby the legislative powers, incapable of annihilation, have returned to the people at large for their exercise, the state remaining, in the meantime, exposed to all the dangers of invasion from without and convulsions within.

He has endeavored to prevent the population of these states; for that purpose obstructing the laws for naturalization of foreigners, refusing to pass others to encourage their migrations hither, and raising the conditions of new appropriations of lands.

He has OBSTRUCTED [*suffered*] the administration of justice BY [*totally to cease in some of these states*] refusing his assent to laws for establishing judiciary powers.

He has made [*our*] judges dependent on his will alone for the tenure of their offices, and the amount and payment of their salaries.

He has erected a multitude of new offices, [*by a self-assumed power*] and sent hither swarms of new officers to harass our people and eat out their substance.

He has kept among us in times of peace standing armies [*and ships of war*] without the consent of our legislatures.

He has affected to render the military independent of, and superior to, the civil power.

He has combined with others to subject us to a jurisdiction foreign to our constitutions and unacknowledged by our laws, giving his assent to their acts of pretended legislation for quartering large bodies of armed troops among us; for protecting them by a mock trial from punishment for any murders which they should commit on the inhabitants of these states; for cutting off our trade with all parts of the world; for imposing taxes on us without our consent; for depriving us IN MANY CASES of the benefits of trial by jury; for transporting us beyond seas to be tried for pretended offences; for abolishing the free system of English laws in a neighboring province, establishing therein an arbitrary government, and enlarging its boundaries, so as to render it at once an example and fit instrument for introducing the same absolute rule into these COLONIES [*states*]; for taking away our charters, abolishing our most valuable laws, and altering fundamentally the forms of our governments; for suspending our own legislatures, and declaring themselves invested with power to legislate for us in all cases whatsoever.

He has abdicated government here BY DECLARING US OUT OF HIS PROTECTION, AND WAGING WAR AGAINST US [*withdrawing his governors, and declaring us out of his allegiance and protection*].

He has plundered our seas, ravaged our coasts, burnt our towns, and destroyed the lives of our people.

He is at this time transporting large armies of foreign mercenaries to complete the works of death, desolation and tyranny already begun with circumstances of cruelty and perfidy SCARCELY PARALLELED IN THE MOST BARBAROUS AGES, AND TOTALLY unworthy the head of a civilized nation.

He has constrained our fellow citizens taken captive on the high seas, to bear arms against their country, to become the executioners of their friends and brethren, or to fall themselves by their hands.

He has EXCITED DOMESTIC INSURRECTION AMONG US, AND HAS endeavored to bring on the inhabitants of our frontiers, the merciless Indian savages, whose known rule of warfare is an undistinguished destruction of all ages, sexes and çonditions [*of existence*].

[*He has incited treasonable insurrections of our fellow citizens, with the allurements of forfeiture and confiscation of our property.*

He has waged cruel war against human nature itself, violating its most sacred rights of life and liberty in the persons of a distant people who never offended him, captivating and carrying them into slavery in another hemisphere, or to incur miserable death in their transportation hither. This piratical warfare, the opprobrium of INFIDEL powers, is the warfare of the CHRISTIAN king of Great Britain. Determined to keep open a market where MEN should be bought and sold, he has prostituted his negative for suppressing every legislative attempt to prohibit or to restrain this execrable commerce. And that this assemblage of horrors might want no fact of distinguished die, he is now exciting those very people to rise in arms among us, and to purchase that liberty of which he has deprived them, by murdering the people on whom he also obtruded them: thus paying off former crimes committed against thé LIBERTIES of one people, with crimes which he urges them to commit against the LIVES of another.]

In every stage of these oppressions we have petitioned for redress in the most humble terms: our repeated petitions have been answered only by repeated injuries.

A prince whose character is thus marked by every act which may define a tyrant is unfit to be the ruler of a FREE people [*who mean to be free. Future ages will scarcely believe that the hardiness of one man adventured, within the short compass of twelve years only, to lay a foundation so broad and so undisguised for tyranny over a people fostered and fixed in principles of freedom.*]

Nor have we been wanting in attentions to our British brethren. We have warned them from time to time of attempts by the legislature to extend AN UNWAR-RANTABLE [a] jurisdiction over US [these our states]. We have reminded them of the circumstances of our emigration and settlement here, [no one of which could warrant so strange a pretension: that these were effected at the expense of our blood and treasure, unassisted by the wealth or the strength of Great Britain: that in con-stituting indeed our several forms of government, we had adopted one common king, thereby laying a founda-tion for perpetual league and amity with them: but that submission to their parliament was no part of our con-stitution, nor ever in idea, if history may be credited: and,] we HAVE appealed to their native justice and magnanimity AND WE HAVE CONJURED THEM BY [as well as to] the ties of our common kindred to disavow these usurpations which WOULD INEVI-TABLY [were likely to] interrupt our connection and correspondence. They too have been deaf to the voice of justice and of consanguinity. WE MUST THERE-FORE [and when occasions have been given them, by the regular course of their laws, of removing from their councils the disturbers of our harmony, they have, by their free election, re-established them in power. At this very time too, they are permitting their chief magistrate to send over not only soldiers of our common blood, but Scotch and foreign mercenaries to invade and de-stroy us. These facts have given the last stab to agoniz-ing affection, and manly spirit bids us to renounce for-ever these unfeeling brethren. We must endeavor to forget our former love for them, and hold them as we hold the rest of mankind, enemies in war, in peace friends. We might have a free and a great people to-gether; but a communication of grandeur and of free-dom, it seems, is below their dignity. Be it so, since *they will have it. The road to happiness and to glory is open to us, too. We will tread it apart from them, and]* acquiesce in the necessity which denounces our [*eternal*] separation AND HOLD THEM AS WE HOLD THE REST OF MANKIND, ENEMIES IN WAR, IN PEACE FRIENDS!

[1] We therefore the representatives of the United States of America in General Congress assembled, do in the name, and by the authority of the good people of these [*states reject and renounce all allegiance and subjection to the kings of Great Britain and all others who may hereafter claim by, through or under them; we utterly dissolve all political connection which may heretofore have subsisted between us and the people or parliament of Great Britain: and finally we do assert and declare these colonies to be free and independent states,*] and that as free and independent states, they have full power to levy war, conclude peace, contract alliances, establish commerce, and to do

We, therefore, the representatives of the United States of America in General Congress assembled, appealing to the supreme judge of the world for the rectitude of our intentions, do in the name, and by the authority of the good people of these colonies, solemnly publish and declare, that these united colonies are, and of right ought to be free and independent states; that they are absolved from all allegiance to the British crown, and that all political connections between them and the state of Great Britain is, and ought to be, totally dissolved; and that as free and independent states, they have full power to levy war, conclude peace, contract alliances, establish commerce, and to do

---

[1] In this closing section, where additions and deletions have been lengthy, Jefferson's device of printing his version in the left column, and the final adopted text in the right column, has been followed.

all other acts and things which independent states may of right do.

And for the support of this declaration, we mutually pledge to each other our lives, our fortunes, and our sacred honor.

all other acts and things which independent states may of right do.

And for the support of this declaration, with a firm reliance on the protection of divine providence, we mutually pledge to each other our lives, our fortunes, and our sacred honor.

JOHN HANCOCK

New Hampshire
JOSIAH BARTLETT,
WM. WHIPPLE,
MATTHEW THORNTON.

Massachusetts-Bay
SAML. ADAMS,
JOHN ADAMS,
ROBT. TREAT PAINE,
ELBRIDGE GERRY.

Rhode Island
STEP. HOPKINS,
WILLIAM ELLERY.

Connecticut
ROGER SHERMAN,
SAM'EL HUNTINGTON,
WM. WILLIAMS,
OLIVER WOLCOTT.

New York
WM. FLOYD,
PHIL. LIVINGSTON,
FRANS. LEWIS,
LEWIS MORRIS.

New Jersey
RICHD. STOCKTON,
JNO. WITHERSPOON,
FRAS. HOPKINSON,
JOHN HART,
ABRA. CLARK.

Pennsylvania
ROBT. MORRIS,
BENJAMIN RUSH,
BENJA. FRANKLIN,
JOHN MORTON,
GEO. CLYMER,
JAS. SMITH,
GEO. TAYLOR,
JAMES WILSON,
GEO. ROSS.

Delaware
CAESAR RODNEY,
GEO. READ,
THO. MCKEAN.

Maryland
SAMUEL CHASE,
WM. PACA,
THOS. STONE,
CHARLES CARROLL of
  Carrollton.

Virginia
GEORGE WYTHE,
RICHARD HENRY LEE,
TH. JEFFERSON,
BENJA. HARRISON,
THS. NELSON, JR.,
FRANCIS LIGHTFOOT
  LEE,
CARTER BRAXTON.

North Carolina
WM. HOOPER,
JOSEPH HEWES,
JOHN PENN.

South Carolina
EDWARD RUTLEDGE,
THOS. HEYWARD, JUNR.,
THOMAS LYNCH, JUNR.,
ARTHUR MIDDLETON.

Georgia
BUTTON GWINNETT,
LYMAN HALL,
GEO. WALTON.

HISTORICAL NOTE
BY THE AUTHORS

The first question we are asked by those who have seen
—or read—*1776* is invariably: "Is it true? Did it really
happen that way?"

The answer is: Yes.

Certainly a few changes have been made in order to
fulfill basic dramatic tenets. To quote a European
dramatist friend of ours, "God writes lousy theater."
In other words, reality is seldom artistic, orderly, or
dramatically satisfying; life rarely provides a sound second act, and its climaxes usually have not been ade-
quately prepared for. Therefore, in historical drama,
a number of small licenses are almost always taken
with strictest fact, and those in *1776* are enumerated in
this addendum. But none of them, either separately or
in accumulation, has done anything to alter the historical truth of the characters, the times, or the events of
American independence.

First, however, let us list those elements of our play
that have been taken, unchanged and unadorned, from
documented fact.

The weather in Philadelphia that late spring and early
summer of 1776 was unusually hot and humid, resulting
in a bumper crop of horseflies incubated in the stable
next door to the State House (now Independence Hall).

John Adams was indeed "obnoxious and disliked"
—the description is his own.

Benjamin Franklin, the oldest member of the Congress, suffered from gout in his later years and often "drowsed" in public.

Thomas Jefferson, the junior member of the Virginia delegation, was entrusted with the daily weather report.

Rhode Island's Stephen Hopkins, known to his colleagues as "Old Grape and Guts" because of his fondness for distilled refreshment, always wore his round black, wide-brimmed Quaker's hat in the chamber.

Portly Samuel Chase, the gourmand from Maryland (pronounced Mary-land in those times), was referred to (behind his back, of course) as "Bacon-Face."

Connecticut's Roger Sherman always sat apart from his fellow Congressmen, sipping coffee from a saucer-like bowl.

Caesar Rodney of Delaware, suffering from skin cancer, never appeared in public without a green scarf wrapped around his face.

The dress of the Congressmen graduated from the liberal greens, golds, brocades, and laces of the conservative Southerners, to the conservative browns, blacks, mean cloth, and plain linen of the radical New Englanders.

The only two known employees of the Congress were Charles Thomson, secretary, who kept no minutes of the debates (recording only those motions which were passed), and Andrew McNair, custodian and bell-ringer.

A motion concerning Congress's liability for a certain Mr. Melchior Meng's dead mule was debated and approved prior to the motion on independence.

Ben Franklin's illegitimate son William was Royal Governor of New Jersey until he was arrested, in June 1776, and exiled to Connecticut.

The New York delegation abstained on many votes, including the final vote on independence (that tally be-

ing recorded by Mr. Thomson as twelve for, none
against, and one abstaining), though later the New
York Legislature (the members of which "speak very
fast and very loud and nobody pays any attention to
anybody else, with the result that nothing ever gets
done") approved the action after the fact.

George Washington's dispatches arrived on an average of three a day, and almost all of them were "gloomy"
to the point of despair.

The strength of the armed forces under Washington's
command was as dismal as he reported. On May 12,
1776, for instance, the Duty Roster of the Continental
Army listed:

Commissioned officers	589
Non-commissioned officers	722
Present & fit for duty	6,641
Sick but present	547
Sick but absent	352
On furlough	66
On command [A.W.O.L.]	1,122

This was the total strength of the American army.

Edward Rutledge of South Carolina, the youngest
member of the Congress, was the leading proponent of
individual rights for individual states.

The committee to "manage" the Declaration of Independence consisted of five Congressmen: Adams,
Franklin, Roger Sherman, Robert Livingston (of New
York—he wasn't available to sign the Declaration, but
he obligingly sent his cousin, Philip, to affix the powerful family name), and Jefferson. The fifth member had
originally been Richard Lee, the offerer of the motion
of independence, but he subsequently declined in order
to return to Virginia, where he had been proposed for
governor of that "country" (as Virginians referred to
their colony). None of the five members of this committee wanted the assignment of actually writing the

Declaration, and all of them begged off for one personal reason or another. But Jefferson, whom Adams accused of being the finest writer in Congress, possessing "a happy talent for composition and a remarkable felicity of expression," was finally persuaded. Later he recalled that the purpose of the Declaration had been "to place before mankind the common sense of the subject in terms so plain and firm as to command their assent."

Jefferson was, besides being an author, lawyer, farmer, architect, and statesman, a fine violinist. His wife, Martha, a young, beautiful widow of twenty-four when they married, was often praised for her "uncommon singing voice." (She died ten years after their wedding, a full nineteen years before Jefferson inhabited the White House, and he never remarried. The Martha Jefferson who is often listed as First Lady was their daughter.)

Jefferson, during those early years in Congress, was not a loquacious man. Adams remembered him as "the most silent man in Congress. . . . I never heard him utter three sentences together."

Adams knew he would not receive his proper due from posterity. He wrote that "the whole history of this Revolution will be to lie, from beginning to end." And, equally, he knew that Franklin was the stuff of which national legends are built. They would certify that "Franklin did this, Franklin did that, Franklin did some other damned thing. . . . Franklin smote the ground and out sprang George Washington, fully-grown and on his horse. . . . Franklin then electrified him with his miraculous lightning rod and the three of them— Franklin, Washington and the horse—conducted the entire Revolution by themselves."

The seemingly endless list of Congressional committees (and their redundant titles) spoken by Secretary

Thomson at the beginning of Scene 5 are all taken from his own report as it appears in the "Journal of Congress."

The Declaration of Independence was debated by the Congress for three full days. It underwent eighty-six separate changes (and withstood scores of others, including an amendment calling for clear and sovereign "fishing rights") and the deletion of over four hundred words, including a strong condemnation of that "peculiar institution" slavery (accusing King George III of waging "cruel war against human nature itself, violating its most sacred rights of life and liberty in the persons of a distant people who never offended him, carrying them into slavery in another hemisphere . . .") which called for its abolition. This paragraph was removed to placate and appease the Southern colonies and to hold them in the Union.

Jefferson, though a slaveholder himself, declared that "nothing is more certainly written in the Book of Fate than that this people shall be free." And further: "The rights of human nature are deeply wounded by this infamous practice."

The deadlock existing within the Delaware delegation of the mortally ill Caesar Rodney, who, in great pain, had ridden all night from Dover, a distance of some eighty miles, arriving just in time to save the motion on independence from being defeated. His sacrifice was all the more remarkable in view of the fact that by voting for the motion he was abandoning forever all hope of receiving the competent medical treatment of his illness that was available in England; he had become a traitor with a price on his head.

When the motion on independence had passed, John Dickinson of Pennsylvania, the leader of the anti-independence forces (desiring reconciliation with England), refused to sign the Declaration, a document he felt he could not endorse. But, asserting a fidelity to America, he left the Congress to enlist in the Continental Army as a private—though he was entitled to a commission—and served courageously with the Delaware Militia. Some years later he was appointed to the Constitutional Convention, representing Delaware, and returned to Philadelphia to contribute greatly to the writing of that extraordinary document, the United States Constitution.

All these historical facts appear in the play. But there are, as has been stated, many other instances where changes were effected. In all cases, however, we believe they were the result of sound dramatic decisions which were aesthetically, as well as historically, justified.

These changes can be divided into five caterogies: things altered, things surmised, things added, things deleted, and things rearranged. Following are examples of all five categories, plus the reasons for the changes.

Things altered: Of the two main alterations that were made, one was in the interest of dramatic construction, the other for the purpose of preserving dramatic unity.

First, the Declaration, though reported back to Congress for amendments and revisions prior to the vote on independence on July 2, was not actually debated and approved until after that vote. However, had this schedule been preserved in the play, the audience's interest in the debate would already have been spent.

Second, the Declaration was not signed on July 4, 1776, the date it was proclaimed to the citizenry of the thirteen colonies. It was actually signed over a period of several months, many of the signers having not been present at the time of its ratification. The greatest number signed on August 2, but one, Matthew Thornton of New Hampshire, did not even enter Congress until November 4, and the name of Colonel Thomas McKean of Delaware, probably the last to sign, had not yet appeared on the document by the middle of January 1777. It seems fairly obvious, however, that the depiction of a July 4 signing, like the famous Pine-Savage engraving of this non-event, provides the occasion with form and allows the proper emotional punctuation to the entire spectacle.

Things surmised: Because Secretary Thomson did not keep a proper record of the debates in Congress, and because other chronicles are incomplete in certain key areas, a small number of educated suppositions had to be made in order to complete the story. These were based on consistencies of character, ends logically connected to means, and the absence of other possible explanations.

It is unknown, for instance, whether Richard Henry Lee was persuaded to go to the Virginia House of Burgesses in order to secure a motion for independence that could be introduced in Congress, or if he volunteered on his own. Certainly Adams was getting nowhere with his own efforts; he had, on twenty-three separate occasions, introduced the subject of independence to his fellows in Congress, and each time it had failed to be considered. It was also true that whenever an issue needed respectability, the influence of a Virginian was brought to bear. (Virginia was the first colony, and its citizens were regarded as a sort of American aristocracy, an honor that was not betrayed by their leaders. The Virginian Washington was given command of the army, and the Virginian Jefferson was given the assignment of writing the Declaration.) Certainly Franklin would have delighted in appealing to Lee's vanity and deflating Adams' ego at one and the same time, as Scene 2 of the play suggests. But the actual sequence of these events is unknown.

And when Lee returned from Virginia (in Scene 3) a transcript of the debate in Congress on his motion for independence was never recorded. But the positions of individual Congressmen are known, and it was possible to glean phrases, attitudes and convictions from the many letters, memoirs, and other papers that exist in abundance, in order to reconstruct a likely facsimile of this debate. (Stick fights, such as the one occurring between Adams and Dickinson in this scene, were common during Congressional debate, and though there is no report of this particular one, the sight of the two antagonists whacking away at each other certainly would have surprised no one.)

Similarly, a record of the debate on the Declaration was never kept. But in this case there was even more to go on. Jefferson himself, in his autobiography, provided two versions of the document—as originally written and as finally approved. Who was responsible for each individual change is not known, but in most instances convincing conclusions are not too hard to draw. McKean, a proud Scot, surely would have objected to the charge of "Scotch & foreign mercenaries [sent] to invade and deluge us in blood." And John Witherspoon of New Jersey, a clergyman and the Congressional chaplain, no doubt would have supported the addition of the phrase "with a firm Reliance on the Protection of Divine Providence," which had not been present in Jefferson's original draft. Also, Edward Rutledge must be charged with leading the fight against the condemnation of slavery, being the chief proponent of that practice in Congress. And the exchange between Jefferson and Dickinson, occurring in our version of this debate, includes lines written by Jefferson on other occasions, most notably: "The right to be free comes from Nature."

The conversion of James Wilson of Pennsylvania from the "Nay" to the "Yea" column at the last minute (in Scene 7) is an event without any surviving explanation.

All that is definitely known is that Wilson, a former law student of Dickinson's and certainly under his influence in Congress, as his previous voting record testifies, suddenly changed his position on independence and, as a result, is generally credited with casting the vote that decided this issue. But why? A logical solution to this mystery was found when we imagined one fear he might have possessed that would have been stronger than his fear of Dickinson's wrath—the fear of going down in history as the man who singlehandedly prevented American independence. Such a position would have been totally consistent with his well-known penchant for caution.

The final logical conjecture we made concerned the discrepancy between the appearance of the word "inalienable" in Jefferson's version of the Declaration and its reappearance as *"un*alienable" in the printed copy that is now in universal use. This could have been a misprint, but it might, too, have been the result of interference by Adams (he had written it as "unalienable" in a copy of the Declaration he had drafted in his own hand), who believed that this seldom-used spelling was correct. There is no doubt that the meddlesome "Massachusettensian," a Harvard graduate, was not above speaking to Mr. Dunlap, the printer.

It is also consistent with both men's behavior that Adams and Jefferson should have disagreed on this matter, as they did on most. They were to become bitter enemies for much of their lives, only to make up when they had both survived to extreme old age. Both lived long enough to be invited (by Adams' son, John Quincy, who was then occupying the White House) to the fiftieth anniversay celebration of the Declaration of Independence. But on that very date, July 4, 1826, exactly a half-century later to the day, both of these gigantic figures, Jefferson at eighty-three, Adams at ninety-one—each believing and finding solace in the thought that the other was attending the jubilee—died. Surely this was one of the greatest coincidences in all history and one which never would be believed if included in a play.

Things added: The three instances of elements that were added to the story of American independence were created in the interest of satisfying the musical-comedy form. Again, it must be stressed that none of them interferes with historic truth in any way.

The first concerns Martha Jefferson's visit to Philadelphia in Scene 4. While it is true that Jefferson missed her to distraction, more than enough to effect an unscheduled reunion, it is believed that he journeyed to Virginia to see her. The license of having her come to see him, at Adams' instigation, stemmed from our desire to show something of the young Jefferson's personal life without destroying the unity of setting.

Second, in Scene 5 of the play, Adams, Franklin, and Chase are shown leaving for New Brunswick, New Jersey, for an inspection of the military. This particular trip did not actually take place, though a similar one was made to New York after the vote on independence, during which Adams and Franklin had to share a single bed in an inn. Originally the New Jersey junket was included in the play, represented by two separate scenes (one in an inn, showing the sleeping arrangements mentioned, the other on the military training grounds, showing inspection of "a ragtag collection of provincial militiamen and irregulars" who could do nothing right until a flock of ducks flew by; the men's hunger molded them into a smoothly operating unit). These scenes were removed, however, during the out-of-town tryout, in the interests of the over-all length of the play and because they were basically cinemagraphic in concept. Needless to say, both should appear in the filmed version of *1776.*

And third, the account of General Washington's dusty young courier, at the end of Scene 5, of a battle he had witnessed, while an actual description of the village green during and after the Battle of Lexington, is a wholly constructed moment, designed to illustrate the feelings and experiences of the Americans outside Congress, who were deeply influenced by the decisions made inside the Congress.

One further note: The tally board used throughout the play to record each vote did not exist in the actual chamber in Philadelphia. It has been included in order to clarify the positions of the thirteen colonies at any given moment, a device allowing the audience to follow the parliamentary action without confusion.

Things deleted: Certain elements that are historically true have been left out of or removed from the play for one of three separate reasons.

The first of these was the embarrassment of riches; there are just too many choice bits of information to include in one, two, or even a dozen plays. The fact that Franklin often entered the Congressional chamber in a sedan chair carried by convicts, for instance; or that, on several occasions, Indians in full regalia would appear before the Congress, petitioning for one thing or another, and accompanied by their interpreter, a full-blooded Indian who spoke with a flawless Oxford accent.

Then there was the advisability of cutting down on the number of Congressmen appearing in the play in the interests of preserving clarity and preventing overcrowding. There is, after all, a limit to an audience's ability to assimilate (and keep separate) a large number of characters, as well as the physical limits of any given stage production. For this reason several of the lesser

known (and least contributory) Congressmen were
eliminated altogether, and in a few cases two or more
were combined into a single character. James Wilson,
for example, contains a few of the qualities of his fellow Pennsylvanian, John Morton. And John Adams is,
at times, a composite of himself and his cousin Sam
Adams, also of Massachusetts.

But by far the most frustrating reason for deleting a
historical fact was that the audiences would never have
believed it. The best example of this is John Adams'
reply (it was actually Cousin Sam who said it) to
Franklin's willingness to drop the anti-slavery clause
from the Declaration. "Mark me, Franklin," he now
says in Scene 7, "if we give in on this issue, posterity
will never forgive us." But the complete line, spoken in
July 1776, was "If we give in on this issue, *there will be
trouble a hundred years hence;* posterity will never forgive us." And audiences would never forgive *us.* For
who could blame them for believing that the phrase was
the author's invention, stemming from the eternal wis-
dom of hindsight? After all, the astonishing prediction
missed by only a few years.

Things rearranged: Some historical data have been
edited dramatically without altering their validity or
factuality.

The first example of this would be the play's treatment of Adams' relationship with his wife, Abigail. Two
separate theatrical conventions have been employed; the
selection and conversion of sections of their actual letters,
written to each other during this period of their separation, into dialogue; and the placing of them in close physical proximity though they remain, in reality, over three
hundred miles apart. The notion for this last device
sprang, oddly, from a line in one of these same letters:
Adams was complaining about their continued separation and finally pleaded, "Oh, if I could only annihilate

time and space!" (The description of scenes, at the beginning of the play, defines these meetings by listing the area of dramatic action as "certain reaches of John Adams' mind.")

The exchanges, spoken and sung, between John and Abigail Adams are, as has been stated, the result of distributing, as dialogue, sections and phrases from various letters. The list of their children's diseases, the constant requests for "saltpetre for gunpowder" (and the counter-request for pins), the use of the tender salutation "Dearest friend," the catalogue of Abigail's faults, the news of the farm in Braintree failing—even certain song lyrics transferred intact ("I live like a nun in a cloister" and "Write to me with sentimental effusion")—all these were edited and rearranged in an attempt to establish a dramatically satisfying relationship.

This same process was used to construct George Washington's dispatches from the field. Literally dozens were selected, from which individual lines were borrowed and then patched together in order to form the five communiqués that now appear in the play. Therefore, though the dispatches as now constructed were not written by the Commander-in-Chief, each sentence within them is either an actual quotation ("O how I wish I had never seen the Continental Army! I would have done better to retire to the back country and live in a wigwam") or paraphrase, or comes from a firsthand report (the final line of the last dispatch, ". . . but dear God! what brave men I shall lose before this business ends!" was spoken by Washington in the presence of his adjutant, who later reported it).

And finally, John Adams' extraordinary prophecy, made on July 3, 1776, describing the way Independence Day would be celebrated by future generations of Americans and written in a letter to his wife on that date, has been paraphrased and adapted into lyric form for the song "Is Anybody There?" sung by Adams in Scene 7. The original lines are:

> I am apt to believe that it will be celebrated by succeeding generations as the great anniversary festival. It ought to be commemorated as the day of deliverance by solemn acts of devotion to God Almighty. It ought to be solemnized with pomp and parade, with shows, games, sports, guns, bells, bonfires, and illumination, from one end of this continent to the other, from this time forward for evermore.
>
> You will think me transported with enthusiasm, but I am not. I am well aware of the toil and blood and treasure that it will cost us to maintain this Declaration and support and defend these States. Yet, through all the gloom, I can see the rays of ravishing light and glory. I can see that the end is more than worth all the means. And that posterity will triumph in that day's transaction, even although we should rue it, which I trust God we shall not.

We have attempted, in the paragraphs above, to answer the question, "Is it true?" What we cannot answer, however, is how such a question could possibly be asked so often by Americans. What they want to know is whether or not the story of their political origin, the telling of their national legend, is correct as presented. Don't they know? Haven't they ever heard it before? And if not, why not? As we say, it's a question we cannot answer.

There are those who would claim that the schools just don't teach it, and we would have trouble disagreeing with them. The authors of *1776* are both products of the American public-school system—one from the West Coast, the other from the East. Both were better than average students with a deeper than average curiosity about American history. But neither of them was given any more than a perfunctory review of the major events, a roster of a few cardboard characters, and a certain number of jingoistic conclusions.

But what of the arguments, the precedents, the compromises, the personalities, the regional disputes, the perseverance, the courage, the sacrifices, the expediencies? What of the similarities between those times and these (states rights *versus* federal rights; property rights *versus* human rights; privileged rights *versus* civil rights) and the differences (if any)? What of the lessons of the past applied to the problems of the future, for what society can plan a future without an intimate knowledge of its own past?

It is presumptuous of us to assume that *1776* will be able to fill even a portion of this lamentable void (though doubtless no small portion of its success is due to the "new" information it offers); the crime is that it should even have to. The United States owes its citizens, at the very least, an educational system that describes, defines, and explains our own existence.

ACKNOWLEDGMENT

The authors of *1776* wish to express their gratitude to the personnel of the Rare Manuscript Room of the New York Public Library; the New Jersey and Pennsylvania Historical Societies; Princeton University; and the Joint Free Public Library of Morristown and Morris Township, New Jersey, for their patience and cooperation in permitting the holding and examining of many original copies of journals, letters, and other documents pertaining to the events of American independence, and for the indescribable emotions arising therefrom.

SELECT BIBLIOGRAPHY

The following is a list of the research material used in the writing of 1776.

The Adams Papers. Ed. Lyman H. Butterfield. Vols. 1–4, *Diary and Autobiography of John Adams. Vols. 5–6, Adams Family Correspondence.* Cambridge, Mass.: Harvard University Press; 1961, 1963.

Adams–Jefferson Letters: The Complete Correspondence between Thomas Jefferson and Abigail and John Adams. Ed. Lester J. Cappon, 2 vols. Chapel Hill: University of North Carolina Press, 1959.

Correspondence among John Adams, Samuel Adams, and James Warren. Vols. LXXII (1917), LXXIII (1925). Collection, Massachusetts Historical Society, Boston.

The Declaration of Independence: The Evolution of the Text Shown in Facsimilies of Various Drafts by Its Author. Ed. Julian P. Boyd. Washington, D.C.: Library of Congress, 1943.

Documentary History of the American Revolution: Consisting of Letters and Papers Relating to the Contest for Liberty, Chiefly in South Carolina, 1776–1782. Ed. R. W. Gibbes, 3 vols. New York: D. Appleton Company, 1853–1857.

Familiar Letters of John Adams and His Wife, Abigail Adams . . . with a Memoir of Mrs. Adams. Ed. Charles Francis Adams. New York: Hurd and Houghton, 1876.

From the King's Message to Parliament of March 7, 1774, to the Declaration of Independence by the United States. American Archives, Fourth Series, 6 vols. Eds. M. St. Clair Clarke and Peter Force. Washington, D.C., 1837–1846.

John Jay Papers. Special Collection, Columbia University Library, New York.

Journals of the Continental Congress, 1774–1789. Ed. from the original records in the Library of Congress by Worthington Chauncy Ford. 22 vols. Washington, D.C.: Government Printing Office, 1906.

Letters of Members of the Continental Congress. Ed. Edmund C. Burnett. 7 vols. Washington, D.C.: Carnegie Institution, 1921.

Letters of Mrs. Adams, the Wife of John Adams. 3d. ed. Boston: C. C. Little and J. Brown, 1841.

Letters on the American Revolution, 1774–1776. Ed. Margaret W. Willard. Port Washington, N.Y.: Kennikat Press, Inc., 1925.

Letters to and from Caesar Rodney, 1756–1784. Ed. George H. Ryden. Philadelphia: University of Pennsylvania Press, 1933.

Lewis Morris Letters. Collection, Morristown National Historical Park, New Jersey.

New Jersey Gazette (Trenton), 1777.

The Papers of Thomas Jefferson. Ed. Julian P. Boyd, et al. 12 vols. Princeton, N.J.: Princeton University Press, 1950.

Pennsylvania Evening Post, 1776.

Pennsylvania Gazette, 1776.

Pennsylvania Packet, 1775.

Orderly Book, Sir William Howe. Lloyd W. Smith Collection, Morristown National Historical Park, New Jersey.

"Speech of John Dickinson Opposing the Declaration of Independence, 1 July 1776." *Pennsylvania Magazine of History and Biography.* Vol. LVX (Oct., 1941): 458–81.

A Summary of the Returns of the Army under the Command of General George Washington during the Years 1775 and 1776. No. IV, p. 19: Returns of the Army.

Thacher, James A. *A Military journal during the American Revolutionary War, from 1775 to 1783: describing interesting events and Transactions of this Period.* 2d ed. Boston: Cottone and Barnard, 1827.

Writing of George Washington from the Original Manuscript Sources, 1745–1799. Ed. J. C. Fitzpatrick. Vols. II, III, IV, V, VI. Washington, D.C.: U.S. Government Printing Office, 1931–1944.

Becker, Carl L. *The Declaration of Independence: A Study in the History of Political Ideas.* New York: Alfred A. Knopf, 1956.

Bolton, Charles Knowles. *The Private Soldier Under Washington.* New York: Charles Scribner's Sons, 1902.

Bowen, Catherine Drinker. *John Adams and the American Revolution,* Boston: Little, Brown and Company, 1950.

Bowers, Claude G. *The Young Jefferson.* Boston: Houghton Mifflin Company, 1945.

Burnett, Edmund Cody. *The Continental Congress.* New York: The Macmillan Company, 1941.

Donovan, Frank. *Mr. Jefferson's Declaration.* New York: Dodd, Mead and Company, 1968.

Goodrich, Charles A. *Lives of the Signers to the Declaration of Independence.* Philadelphia: DeSilver, 1831.

Haraszti, Zoltan. *John Adams and the Prophets of Progress.* Cambridge, Mass.: Harvard University Press, 1952.

Hendrick, Burton J. *The Lees of Virginia: Biography of a Family.* Boston: Little, Brown and Company, 1935.

Lukens, Jesse. "Letters" in *American Historical Record.* Vol. I: 547–48.

Malone, Dumas. *The Story of the Declaration of Independence.* New York: Oxford University Press, 1954.

Martin, Joseph P. *A Narrative of Some of the Adventures, Dangers and Sufferings of a Revolutionary Soldier.* Hallowell, Me., 1830. Published later as *Private Yankee Doodle.* Ed. George F. Scheer. Boston: Little, Brown and Company, 1962.

Miller, John C. *Origins of the American Revolution.* Boston: Little, Brown and Company, 1943.

Perry, Ralph Barton. *Puritanism and Democracy.* New York: Vanguard Press, Inc., 1914.

Van Doren, Carl. *Benjamin Franklin: A Biography.* New York: The Viking Press, Inc.; 1938, 1956.